## PRAISE FOR *NOT SO FUNNY WHEN IT HAPPENED*

"*Not So Funny When It Happened* is a refreshingly funny book."

—*Publishers Weekly*

"Incredibly funny travel tales."

—*ForeWord*

"A noted travel writer himself, Tim Cahill has collected the best humorous travel pieces in one funny-bone volume."

—*Chicago Tribune*

"An amusing diversion, good for your next long flight."

—*Kirkus Review*

"These stories are humorous, indeed. In a few cases the reader may have gone through a similar agonizing experience—one that was not the least bit funny at the time, but comical to look back on."

—*Booklist*

"An engaging paperback from the enterprising San Francisco travel publisher."

—*San Francisco Chronicle*

"It's a book full of short, funny, glad-it-didn't-happen-to-me stories sure to amuse those who enjoy writing or traveling, or both."

—*Tennessean*

"A delightful, often laugh-out-loud collection of traumatic travel tales."

—*Times-Picayune*

## Other Travelers' Tales Humor Titles

Sand in My Bra

Whose Panties Are These?

The Thong Also Rises

What Color is Your Jockstrap?

Hyenas Laughed at Me and Now I Know Why

Last Trout in Venice

There's No Toilet Paper on the Road Less Traveled

TRAVELERS' TALES

# not so funny when it happened

THE BEST of travel humor and misadventure

TRAVELERS' TALES

# so funny when it happened

THE BEST of travel humor and misadventure

EDITED BY TIM CAHILL

*Series Editors*

James O'Reilly and Larry Habegger

Travelers' Tales
Palo Alto

**Not So Funny When It Happened:**
**The Best of Travel Humor and Misadventure**
Edited by Tim Cahill



*Cover design: Stefan Gutermuth*
*Interior design: Kathryn Heflin and Susan Bailey*
*Cover photograph: Copyright © Desmond Boylan/Reuters*
*Page layout by Patty Holden, using the fonts Bembo, Journal Text, Onyx, and Lithos*

Distributed by Publishers Group West, 1700 Fourth Street, Berkeley, California 94710.

Library of Congress Cataloguing-in-Publication Data

Not so funny when it happened : the best of travel humor and misadventure / edited by Tim Cahill.
p. cm. — (Travelers tales)
Originally published: 2000.
Includes index.
ISBN-13: 978-1-932361-44-5 (pbk.)
ISBN-10: 1-932361-44-8
1. Travel—Anecdotes. 2. Travel—Humor. I. Cahill, Tim.
G151.N68 2006
910.4—dc22

2006022570

Printed in the United States
10 9 8 7 6 5 4 3 2 1

*There are certain queer times and occasions in this strange mixed affair we call life when a man takes his whole universe for a vast practical joke.*

—Herman Melville

# *Table of Contents*


*Introduction* — *xiii*
TIM CAHILL

How I Killed Off My Ex-Wife — 1
JOHN WOOD
*Vietnam*

Hold On to Your Lunch — 7
ELLIOTT NEAL HESTER
*Airborne*

Everybody's Got Glorious Hide Next to Me and My Monkey — 13
JAYCE WHITE
*Zimbabwe*

The Aunties — 20
ANNE LAMOTT
*Mexico*

Jesus Shaves — 28
DAVID SEDARIS
*Paris*

*Benvenuto in Italia!* — 34
SOURAV SEN
*Italy*

Mexican Mating Calls — 39
GERMAINE W. SHAMES
*Mexico*

What's Cooking? — 43
BILL BRYSON
*Vermont*

The Dentist in Cameroon 48
NIGEL BARLEY
*Cameroon*

The Crafty Cousin 52
WILLIAM DALRYMPLE
*Syria*

Incident at San Antonio 55
LUIS ALBERTO URREA
*Mexico*

A Train, a Frog, and Aliens 59
RANDY WAYNE WHITE
*USA*

They Tell Me You Are Big 78
TODD McEWEN
*Chicago*

The Transit Lounge Shuffle 82
DOUGLAS ADAMS AND MARK CARWARDINE
*Tanzania*

The King of the Ferret-Leggers 86
DONALD KATZ
*England*

What I Did in the Doll House 95
SEAN O'REILLY
*Massachusetts*

The Copenhagen T-Shirt 98
THOM ELKJER
*Denmark*

The Rodent 107
MARK SALZMAN
*China*

It's a Man's World 111
LYNN FERRIN
*Yosemite*

Penny Pinched 115
ROLF POTTS
*Thailand*

Called on the Carpet in Marrakech 124
JOHN FLINN
*Morocco*

Passing the Test in Silverton 129
GARY A. WARNER
*Australia*

The Fox Hunt 136
J. P. DONLEAVY
*Ireland*

The Reluctant Chef and Her Rainbow Special 143
CARA TABACHNICK
*Guatemala*

The Elephant that Roared 148
CLEO PASKAL
*Faroe Islands, North Atlantic*

Speaking in Tongues 152
TIM CAHILL
*California*

Show Me the Money 161
BRAD NEWSHAM
*San Francisco*

Welcome to Ireland 165
DAVE BARRY
*Ireland*

Bad Haircuts Around the World 169
DOUG LANSKY
*Asia and South America*

Fear of Not Flying 174
ADAIR LARA
*San Francisco*

April Fool 178
NICHOLAS DELBANCO
*France*

Mr. Disguise 181
RICHARD STERLING
*Vietnam*

Close Encounters of the California Kind 185
MICHAEL LANE AND JIM CROTTY
*California*

A Past Life 194
BURLEY PACKWOOD
*India*

*Index of Contributors* 201
*Acknowledgments* 203

# *Not So Funny When It Happened:* An Introduction

TIM CAHILL

Ladies and gentlemen, laugh if you will, at this sincere and earnest collection of twisted travel narratives. I mean O.K., O.K., laugh a lot if you'd like: that's the point. But the writers here—I know many of them personally—endured the agonies of frustration, terror, boredom, and furious cultural cross currents (not to mention unmentionable toilets) all to bring us unexpected insights into the human condition, which is the writer's highest calling. Could these fine authors help it if the small part of the human condition that flashed before them in their various torments just happened to be funnier than the time grandma sat on the fart cushion? No, they could not. But, hey, what is hilarious now, was, for the most part, anguish at the time, which is to say, most of what you read here was not so funny when it happened.

This concept—the strange unity of travel writing, the hilarity of the human condition, and fart cushions—arose out of a long running conversation I've had over the years with Larry Habegger, who is the big cheese editor of Travelers' Tales. We both believe that some of the best and most perceptive travel writing is also often some of the funniest. I thought a Travelers' Tales anthology of humorous travel stories would prove the point.

Some years later, as it happened, Larry sent me a collection of travel narratives he and other Travelers' Tales editors had selected. They had chosen some familiar but timeless classics; they included stories by the usual culprits (Dave

Barry, Anne Lamott, Bill Bryson) along with articles by writers whose work I didn't know. All of it was funny to one degree or another. I suggested some of my personal favorites (works by Don Katz, David Sedaris, Douglas Adams, and Randy White). We banged these ideas—writers and tales—back and forth for months, discarded some worthy pieces, added a few more, and juggled the sequence. Time passed and, by God, we had put together a book.

In the editing process, I've had the opportunity to carefully read *Not So Funny When It Happened* several times. It gets more enjoyable with each pass.

Some of the pieces that originally merely brought a smile to my face will suddenly graduate to laugh-out-loud status while tales that were absolute knee-slappers on first reading begin to yield up important life lessons. Time is funny that way.

On a personal note: I have included a story of my own, but asked Larry and the editors of Travelers' Tales to choose which one. I was a little surprised by their selection, because, in fact, I very vividly recall the experience related. It was one fraught with terror, a lot of frustration, a good deal of cultural cross currents, and of course, unmentionable toilets. It really was not so funny when it happened.

JOHN WOOD

# How I Killed Off My Ex-Wife

*...and would gladly do it again.*

"I'M TOURING VIETNAM," I TOLD AN OLD ASIA VETERAN. "Any suggestions?"

"Yeah, use mosquito repellent, stay on the trails, and tell everybody you're sorry."

Good advice, as it turned out, but the best tip of all was buried in a guidebook. It warned me that the Vietnamese tend to ask very personal questions, and that the most innocent queries are usually loaded. For example: "Almost every Vietnamese will ask if you are married and have children." True. Every single Vietnamese I met, from cyclo drivers to waiters to shopowners to touts to farmers, asked me that question, usually preceded by "Where are you from?" and "How old are you?" It was as if they'd all been issued a *Fodor's on Foreigners* government manual.

The guidebook cautioned, however, that "telling the Vietnamese you are single or divorced will disturb them greatly. Not having a family is regarded as bad luck, and such people are to be pitied, not envied." Fortunately, the book's authors had a solution: "If you are young and single, simply say you are 'not yet married' and that will be accepted." But I was forty-eight. "If you are over thirty and unmarried, it's better to lie."

Ethically, I have a problem with lying, especially to foreign hosts. Realistically, I have a bigger problem: I am a pitiful liar. What reasoning could have prompted such advice? "Divorce is scandalous," the book concluded. "You'd be better off claiming your former spouse died."

To this day, I don't believe I have ever read a more tawdry, cold-hearted, and insensitive—not to mention brilliant and satisfying—tip in any travel guidebook. Within hours of landing in country, that advice was put to the test. As I stepped onto a boat in the tiny river village of Vinh Long, the starting point for a two-day tour up the Mekong Delta, Mr. Hai, our guide, approached me and asked, "Where you from?" Washington, D.C., I said. Mr. Hai nodded, saying he'd seen pictures of our capital. Very beautiful.

"You how old?" was his second question, just as the handbook had predicted.

I told him, and he shook his head forcefully, saying I appeared much younger.

"You married?" came the third—and most precarious—inquiry. Carefully reciting what I'd memorized before the trip, I explained that I had been married before, but was no longer. Before my words were barely out of my mouth, a light seemed to go out in Mr. Hai's eyes and he replied, more in the form of a conclusion than a question, "Ah...divorce." I took a deep breath, put on my most sorrowful expression, and replied, "No...she...died."

It was as if the entire boat had been given a jolt of electricity. Mr. Hai sat down, stricken, his eyes boring into mine with disbelief. He started ringing his hands and mumbling, "Pity, pity, pity. I sorry for you. So sorry."

Geez, what kind of advice had that been? This poor man was grieving for someone who, if I knew my ex-wife at all, was probably shopping at Nordstrom at that moment. He leaned forward suddenly, and I thought he was having a seizure. "How she die?" he asked softly.

Excuse me? Apparently, the Vietnamese have no expression for "curiosity killed the cat." (Or maybe that's what killed them; I only saw two cats during the two weeks I was in Vietnam. But that's another story.) I hadn't prepared any other answers, so I blurted out "Accident."

Unwise. If my initial news had saddened Mr. Hai, this put him in near hypoxia. He struggled to find words, failed, and his hands covered his face. I tried to look as tormented as I could, which was becoming less and less difficult under the circumstances. He wanted to say something to me. He was determined to get it out. I bent forward to comfort him. At last, he spoke.

"What kind of accident?"

I made a vow at that moment to write a scathing letter when I got home to the author of the guidebook, its editor, its publisher, and every member of their families. I told Mr. Hai my wife perished in a car accident, hoping that would end the conversation. Although *he* nearly perished at the news, the interrogation continued.

"You have children?"

I have a stepson. Rather than muddy the waters with that, I simply said I had a son. I was gratified to see that was just the antidote Mr. Hai needed. He recovered within seconds and asked if I had a picture. Not thinking, I unconsciously took it out of my wallet and showed it to him. He took it carefully in both hands and showed it to his boat driver, and they both beamed. Then he asked, "You have picture of wife?"

I stared at him. For at least twenty or thirty minutes. My body and brain had locked up. "No," was all I could say. Which is true, I no longer carry my ex-wife's picture, although she still carries mine. But that's another story, too.

"You no have picture of wife?" Mr. Hai was aghast. The boat driver's eyes were as big as saucers. They were also looking at me instead of downriver, which had caused our boat to veer sharply toward an oncoming barge of ducks.

"I used to carry her picture," I sputtered in the most woeful tone I could muster. "But after the tragedy, whenever I looked at it...I would cry." Mr. Hai bowed his head and clutched my arm. I bowed my head and clutched my stomach; I think I was having a stress attack.

Thankfully, our boat docked at that moment before my little water-puppet drama—and my bowels—unraveled any further. During the next two weeks, this dialogue was repeated verbatim with literally dozens of other Vietnamese. I have no idea whether any of them believed my lamentable story, but each and every one reacted the same way Mr. Hai did.

Except for one person.

"You did *what*?"

"I killed you off," I told my ex-wife when I got back.

"Normally, I resist inquiring about your odd behavior. But this time it seems to have become personal. So amuse me. Why did you kill me off?"

"I didn't want to offend the Vietnamese."

"I see. That sounds perfectly logical and makes absolutely no sense. Just like you. You know, on second thought, I don't really want an explanation—"

"Good, because I don't think I could—"

"How?"

"Excuse me?"

"How did you kill me off?"

"You really don't want to go there. Look, it's the thought that counted. I'll explain it all some day."

"You'll tell me now or I'll pester you until you do."

"Well, the problem is, the story kept changing each time I told it. You know that old party game where each person repeats the same story to the person next to him, but they all end up exaggerating—"

"Out with it."

"Okay. An earthquake knocked your car off the freeway, you landed in the middle of a race riot, and you were beaten up by LAPD officers."

"Cool. That's so L.A."

"Uh, well, there's more. A forest fire forced them to evacuate you from the hospital, a rainstorm put out the fire, but it caused a mudslide, which washed you away."

"So glad you didn't overdo the clichés. I assume I passed away then?"

"Er, no. You managed to drag yourself onto the 18th green of the Bel Air Country Club and called for help. Unfortunately, your disturbance caused one of the golfers to miss a match-winning three-foot putt."

"That's how I died? How anticlimactic."

"O. J. was putting."

*John Wood has gotten into trouble in nearly every country he's visited. Most of his adventures, he proudly admits, have come from inventiveness and stupidity, not travel guidebooks.*

*

How could I foresee a visit to an obscure archaeological site in Vietnam would one day jeopardize my domestic life?

It so happened that on one of my trips I met a girl, who became my wife. As I was working overseas, she came over to join me there and settle down for what seemed a life of marital bliss. However, one day she was cleaning up some old papers I kept stashed away in a desk. Among them was a fax I had sent a few years before to a travel agent in Da Nang, Vietnam, in preparation of one of my trips. In this fax I explained that, being interested in local history, I wanted to see the ruins of the long-lost Champa Empire. These are located in central Vietnam, in a place called Mee Sun. However, in Vietnamese this is spelled "My Son." So my fax contained the sentence: "Also I would like to visit My Son!"

When I came home that evening I was received by a fuming mad spouse. Shoving the accusing piece of paper in my face, she demanded, in no uncertain terms, an explanation. After reading it I couldn't help bursting out in laughter. But it took quite some effort to convince her that I was not hiding a secret past or leading a double life.

—Carool Kersten, "My Son in Vietnam"

ELLIOTT NEAL HESTER

* * *

# Hold On to Your Lunch

*Sometimes turbulence is just the beginning of a flight attendant's problems.*

DURING THE FINAL TWENTY MINUTES OF A NINE-HOUR ALL-nighter from Rio de Janeiro to Miami, I came face to face with an unspeakable horror. It was about 5 A.M. The cabin was dark, save for a few passenger reading lamps and a dim glow from the main-cabin galley where I was busy completing the liquor inventory.

As I locked the last of the service carts, a young kid stumbled into the galley. He was about eight years old, with big doll-like eyes that blinked sluggishly beneath his wrinkled brow. He frowned and held his belly in both hands.

"What's the matter?" I asked.

"I don't feeeeel good," he said. He spoke in a soft, reedy voice that would have melted the hearts of my co-workers had they not retreated into the lavatories to freshen up before landing.

My heart didn't melt, however. I took two steps backward, worried that the kid would puke on my shoes.

"Where are your parents?" I demanded.

"Sleeeeeping."

"Do you need to go to the bathroom?" (I said this while nodding vigorously and pointing to the nearest lavatory.)

"Nooooo."

"Hmmmm...I guess your tummy hurts, huh?"

"Yesssss," he said.

I sat him on the jump seat while I searched for some ginger ale to help settle his stomach. He stared sullenly into space, rocking, with both arms wrapped around his waist.

By the time I turned back to give him the glass of ginger ale, his eyes seemed to have grown to twice their original size. There was a look of blatant surprise on his face—the comical expression of a boy who, upon hearing his father tumble down the stairs, suddenly remembered where he'd left his toy fire engine. His eyes grew even wider. His lips pursed. His cheeks swelled to Dizzy Gillespie proportions. But this kid was preparing to blow something other than air into a trumpet.

In thirteen years as a flight attendant I've seen more than my fair share of air sickness. I once saw a drunken couple take turns barfing into each other's lap, as if playing a sickly version of "Can You Top That." I watched a Catholic priest vomit into the face of his secular seatmate. I watched a teenage girl open the seat-back pocket in front of her and proceed to fill it with the contents of her stomach. I watched a queasy businessman splatter the last row of passengers after an ill-fated sprint toward the lavatory.

In one particularly memorable episode that triggered a chain reaction of in-flight regurgitation, I watched the volcanic eruption of a 300-pound vacationer who'd eaten three servings of lasagna. After witnessing this spectacle (and inhaling the pungent odor that wafted through the cabin in its wake), more than two dozen passengers leaned into the aisle and retched. Gallons of heavy liquid splashed onto the carpet; even if you closed your eyes you could not escape the sound. Or the smell. I still get queasy just thinking about it.

Throughout all these years of high-altitude nausea there is one consolation, however. Though I've dumped enough air-sick bags to fill an Olympic-size pool, though my olfactory gland has been violated far beyond the limits of rational expectation, though I've sprinkled more puke-absorbent coffee grounds than Maxwell House would care to know, I have never been splattered by a single drop of vomitus.

But now, an eight-year-old kid with bulging eyes and a high-octane stomach was aiming his nozzle directly at me.

In the split-second that I realized he was about to explode, I dived to one side like a stunt man in a Schwarzenegger flick. I hit the floor, rolled once, and came to rest against the aft right-hand exit door. From this relatively safe vantage point,

The farther from central Russia, the stranger the flights often become. On a desert runway between the central Asian capitals of Ashkhabad and Dushanbe, the cabin temperature hovered above 100°F. By the time the ancient, prop-driven plane was fully powered up, the engines were screaming in protest and everything was shaking violently. We lumbered down the runway and, holding our breath, somehow became airborne, held aloft apparently by the swarms of flies onboard and the enthusiastic fanning and swatting of the passengers.

—Lee Forsythe,
"Aeroflotsam and Jetsam"

I watched the action unfold in a semidetached, slow-motion blur.

Just before the kid convulsed, he managed to cover his mouth with both hands. But this maneuver seemed to cause more harm than good. Thin sheets of ejecta shot from between his tiny fingers and splattered the face of all four galley ovens. His head proceeded to swing side to side in a 180-degree assault that covered the galley in a yellowish-orange slime.

I stared at him with a mixture of awe and repulsion. It was as if he had become one of those rapid-fire lawn sprinklers with the rotating mechanical head. The Lawn Boy 2000: We guarantee maximum saturation or your money back! The stuff just kept coming and coming and coming.

After what seemed like an eternity, the kid finally ran out of juice. Literally. With one half-hearted swipe of his sleeve, he wiped his chin, then turned to look at me. His eyes had returned to normal size. But now they were heavy, weighed down by guilt and embarrassment. His spew-covered hands began to tremble as tears ran down his cheeks.

Watching this display of raw kiddie emotion, my hardened heart loosened a bit. Fighting the stench that was beginning to make me dizzy, I rose to my feet and stepped toward the kid, careful to avoid the pools of ooze that covered much of the galley floor.

As I approached, he began to cry in earnest. Big boo-hoo sobs. He just sat there, bawling, covered from head to toe in liquefied airplane cuisine.

Overcome by a paternal urge to pat him on the shoulder, but unable to find an adequate dry spot, I reached out with one finger and sort of ruffled his hair a bit. He looked up at me wearing an expression that, for a moment, tugged at the heartstrings of forgiveness. Then the unthinkable happened.

Much like that infamous scene from *The Exorcist*, the kid looked right into my eyes and let loose a Linda Blair pea-soup blast that covered me from the knees down to the tips of my uniform shoes. I stood there, motionless, feeling the molten bile seep through my socks and into the gaps between my toes.

Before I could throttle the kid he leapt from the jump seat and disappeared into the darkened cabin.

*Elliott Hester was a flight attendant for fifteen years before taking a sabbatical to travel and write. His work has appeared in* National Geographic Traveler, Men's Fitness, Glamour, Maxim, Endless Vacation, *Salon.com, and other publications. He is the author of* Adventures of a Continental Drifter *and* Plane Insanity: A Flight Attendant's Tales of Sex, Rage and Queasiness at 30,000 Feet, *from which this story was excerpted.*

*

The Train de Grande Vitesse bound for Marseille traveled so smoothly it was difficult to tell that we were moving at all. This smoothness did not diminish as the speed increased and I wondered why trains couldn't be like this back in Blighty. The difference between British and French tracks, I have since discovered, is that the French apparently have "superior technology." This baffles me somewhat. We are not talking about a closely guarded military secret or a tiny piece of microcircuitry in a laboratory, we're talking about lumps of steel nailed to bits of wood, and not only that but we're talking about something that is found in such abundance that I can't imagine anything easier than traveling to France, looking at the track, ascertaining what is different and copying it. However, this is apparently beyond the capabilities of those responsible for the British railway infrastructure, and that's just the way it is.

—Stewart Ferris and Paul Bassett, *Don't Mention the War!: A Shameful European Adventure*

By permission of Dave Coverly and Creators Syndicate.

JAYCE WHITE

# Everybody's Got Glorious Hide Next to Me and My Monkey

*An Australian is brought back to his roots.*

WHEN YOU'RE BROUGHT UP IN AUSTRALIA, YOU'RE COMpletely fearless. The extraordinary fact that you're still alive in what is assuredly the most dangerous place on the planet decorates you with a lion-hearted gallantry to rival the most valiant of mythic dragon slayers. News bulletins are emblazoned with constant reminders that Australia boasts the top ten most poisonous spiders and snakes in the world. Indeed, a typical Thursday night pub conversation would doubtless involve mention of the arachnid hit parade, and the minutiae of a red belly blacksnake's appetite for destruction are scrutinized in football scrums and sewing circles alike. As early as primary school, you'll learn how the cane toad could render you blind from the other side of the playground. We laugh in the face of North America's grizzly bears. You haven't seen grizzly till you've snagged a twenty-foot croc on the end of a short fishing line.

The thing is, you don't come across a hell of a lot of amphibious reptiles through the course of day-to-day life in

Sydney. You don't see cane toads in the classroom or giant bush pigs in the pub, and you don't have to swerve to miss a massacre of cassowaries on the M5 overpass. You live in a totally irrational state of fearlessness. *I* live in a totally irrational state of fearlessness. At least, I did for twenty-six-odd years. It took a savagely foreign environment and a truly bizarre set of circumstances to rekindle that primal, well-adjusted, white-knuckled spinelessness we're all born with. That environment was southern Africa. Those circumstances follow.

A sign on the lion cage at a zoo in the Czech Republic:

NO SMOOTHEN THE LION.

For my good friend Antony—having lived the first four years of his life in Zimbabwe (then Rhodesia)—a return pilgrimage was well overdue. With a reputation for being a bit of a ladies' man, he was determined to leave his indulgent lifestyle and hedonistic routine back in the airport lounge bar and not be content to merely tour the stock post-card sites. His was a mission to explore the real Africa, the wild Africa. Mostly he went looking in nightclubs.

Antony's cousin Michael, a professional hunter, was to be our guide for most of the trip. A true Zimbabwean through and through. A real man's man.

Me, well, I was neither a ladies' man nor a man's man. More your straightforward, run-of-the-mill everyman. Just a regular guy. Joe Average. Smithers Jones. John Q. Citizen. No, I wasn't into credit card fraud—just eking out an existence of utterly soul-destroying, spirit-crushing tedium. Blinded by light so flourescent, suffocated by air so conditioned. So when the opportunity came along to wake up and smell the coffee in a refreshingly unfamiliar surrounding, naturally I seized it with both nostrils.

I woke up in a round thatched hut at Victoria Falls, not to the smell of coffee but to the sound of baboons vandalizing round thatched huts, swinging from light poles, and bashing out industrial dance beats on garbage lids and barbecue amenities. While this is not an experience one would expect from a stay at The Hilton Vienna Plaza, it was a relatively civilized affair. A fridge and a fan by the door, table and chairs in the center, and three beds that dovetailed out to the ever-thinning walls. A steel-framed door with full-length glass panes afforded me the occasional glimpse of a passing primate. I had never felt so at peace, so at one with nature. I had the awesome wonder of creation frolicking just outside my door.

Then it happened.

A baboon the size of an adult wookie pressed his face against the glass—hands shielding the reflected glare of sunrise. Was he looking for Jessica Lange? She wasn't with us. I wished she was, he might have accepted her as a sacrifice and left us alone—a sacrificial Lange. But no, seconds later Chewbacca swings open the door like he owns the place and pulls up a chair at the breakfast table, just centimeters from the foot of my bed. (Now I don't know how many baboon asses you've seen up close, but let me just say that if the folks who ran this establishment showed any sense of social responsibility they'd have burned that chair and buried the remains at the first available opportunity.)

I froze for a moment, gradually started breathing again and tried to collect my thoughts, consider all possibilities. The side effects brought on by malaria tablets I was taking included vivid dreams, but so far these had mostly featured starring roles by one or more Spice Girls, so I was forced to resign myself to the fact that this was probably reality. When Antony stumbled home in a drunken haze an hour or so earlier, he must have forgotten to lock the door behind him (against the ever so vehement advice of the groundsmen) because the awesome wonder of creation was no longer just outside. It was now *inside* and appeared to be dauntlessly feasting on our leftover *spaanspek, sudsa* and *boerewors*. Was it not enough that we should share a substantial portion of our genetic makeup with this hirsute brute? Must we also share equal measures of delicious, albeit scarcely pronounceable, traditional Zimbabwean dishes?

As always, the others were sleeping like tranquilized logs. I pulled myself together and shrieked as politely as possible, "Get out! Go away!... %★@# OFF!"

Well, apparently baboons have little or no understanding of the English language or its affiliated colloquialisms because this one didn't so much as flinch. My emotional fervor did, however, manage to bring Antony into some sort of semiconscious state. "Go back to sleep," he mumbled, not noticing there was someone in the room who had failed to put his $100 Zim share into the accommodation kitty.

"But there's an ape sitting at the table," I whispered so as not to offend our visitor.

There was silence, aside from the devoted munching sounds and my occasional high-pitched yelp. Someone had to take some decisive action. I reached for my Walkman (I was getting sick of that Deep Forest/Enigma compilation tape anyway) and hurled it roughly in Kong's direction. Sadly, the headphones were wrapped around a lamp, a glass of water, and a travel clock, so my projectile stopped well short of its target and an avalanche of paraphernalia came crashing to the floor.

While Michael slept on, Antony was once more distracted from his dreams. His glance turned to me, then following my line of sight, toward our guest. His heavy squint then turned to a wide-eyed gape.

"rrRRRAAAAAAAAAAAAAAAH..." He charged forward, pillow in hand, shouting and waving and swiftly chased the sorry-assed beast out of there. Then, without a word of post-match commentary, went straight back to bed, head gently resting on his implement of warfare—back into Spice World, "ZZZ...ZZZ...ZZZ..."

Michael later told us stories of how baboons have teeth like those of a lion and how they've been known to kill leopards. While it was some comfort to hear this, it didn't change anything. From that day forward I was hyperaware of the coward I really was. I developed fears of peaches, poodles, car seat covers, coconuts, brown suede shoes, and certain varieties of cheese. Basically, anything furrier than Laminex throws me into a frenzied panic attack. The collective drone of mastication in fast-food restaurants sends cold shivers down my spine.

Don't get me wrong, I don't see it as a bad thing at all. In fact, it's given me a new lease on life as I no longer take unnecessary risks. Sleeping with the door barricaded, intoning witch doctor-prescribed hexes on a daily basis, carrying tranquilizer darts at all times. All sensible precautions bestowed upon me by my newfound phobias. I'll probably live decades longer than my pre-baboon-confrontation self could have imagined.

Yes, it was a morning I shall never forget. The tepid air,

the slant of light. And Antony's confused words, just after waking: "Who ate all the *boerewors*?"

*Jayce White was born and raised in Sydney, Australia. Although he has worked in the shadowy corners of the publishing industry for a decade, it was his passion for travel which taught him to write, through countless letters home and to friends gleaned along the way. He has visions of a full-time career as a writer, visual artist, and pop star.*

*

My rather wobbly control of the language was also a grave danger. Obscenity is never very far away in Dowayo [a tribal language in Cameroon]. A shift of tone changes the interrogative particle, attached to the sentence to convert it into a question, into the lewdest word in the language, something like "cunt." I would, therefore, baffle and amuse Dowayos by greeting them, "Is the sky clear for you, cunt?"

But my problems were not exclusively with interrogative vaginas; similar problems haunted eating and copulation. One day I was summoned to the Chief's hut to be introduced to a rainmaker. This was a most valuable contact that I had nagged the Chief about for weeks. We chatted politely, very much sounding each other out. I was not supposed to know he was the rainmaker; I was the one being interviewed. I think he was much impressed by my respectful demeanor. We agreed that I would visit him. I was anxious to leave since I had acquired some meat for the first time in a month and left it in my assistant's care. I rose and shook hands politely, "Excuse me," I said, "I am cooking some meat." At least that was what I had intended to say; owing to tonal error I declared to an astonished audience. "Excuse me. I am copulating with the blacksmith."

—Nigel Barley, *The Innocent Anthropologist: Notes from a Mud Hut*

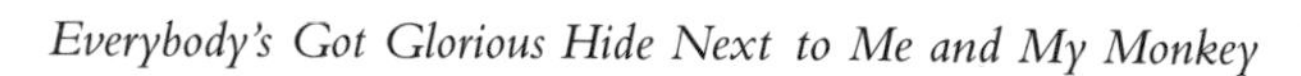

"My boy Kong, he'll be tall and as tough as a tree, will Kong,
Like a tree he'll grow with his head held high and his feet planted firm on the ground,
And ya won't see nobody dare to try to boss him or toss him around. . . ."

Cartoon by Jack Ziegler

ANNE LAMOTT

# The Aunties

*She never leaves home without them.*

SPIRITUAL EXPERIENCES DO NOT HAPPEN FREQUENTLY AT tropical vacation spots for normal people who travel well, but there is no one fitting that description around here. I wish I could get to Kathmandu for my transformations, but I can't get any farther than Mexico. I am too much of an alarmist to stay airborne much longer than that; I can only cross one or two time zones before serious decompensation sets in. I would love to go to the Caribbean someday, or India. But they're too far. In the meantime, Mexico is my training tropics.

So I was in the Mexican state of Oaxaca when I got my most recent brown-bag spiritual victory: I broke through Butt Mind in the town of Huatulco. Or at any rate, I have only had a mild case of Butt Mind since. In earlier incarnations I've spent days and entire weeks comparing my butt to everyone else's butt. Sometimes my butt was better-than, although it is definitely the butt of a mother who keeps forgetting to work out. Mostly it was worse-than. On tropical beaches it has almost always been much-worse-than. I did not expect things to be any different this time, because gravity is having its say. Also as it turned out, there were lots of teenage girls around, only a few of whom, statistically, could be expected to have droopy butts and major dimpling issues—the feta-cheese look, as one friend puts it.

I started off in heavy Butt Mind on the plane. I was with my son Sam and our best friends. There were all these teenage girls on board in tiny shorts that Sam could have borrowed. Someone less secure about her own beauty might have said, "Too many teenage girls." They were mostly youthful and bouncy and physically stunning, if you happen to find tan lean youth attractive. But I had recently read a magazine article on Junkie Chic, society's current exhortation of drowsy, skaggy emaciation. And for some reason the article was *mostly* making me feel militantly on my own middle-aged-mother-butt side.

I was also thinking of a priest I have mentioned before, who said that sometimes he thinks that heaven is just a new pair of glasses. I was trying to remember to wear them. I was trying to spend less time thinking about what I see and more time thinking about why I see it that way—why I continue, off and on, to see these nice sturdy high-functioning thighs with such contempt. It's so troubling to relapse in this area, especially since somewhere along the line, I have actually come to believe that a person being herself is beautiful—that contentment and acceptance and freedom are beautiful. And most important, I have discovered *I* am clinically and objectively beautiful.

I really mean this in the literal sense. I believe that if you saw me, you would say, "Wow! What a beautiful woman."

I think.

I'm almost sure.

But of course, I was thinking all these lofty things before I got to the beach.

Until recently, I was afraid to say that I am beautiful out loud for fear that people would look at each other with amusement and think to themselves, *Well, isn't that nice*. And then they would look at me with cruel scrutiny and see a thinnish woman with tired wrinkly eyes, flabby thighs, scriggly-scraggly hair, as my son once described it, and scriggly-scraggly teeth. I was afraid they would see the spidery veins on my legs and note that my bottom appears to be making a break for freedom from the confines of my swimsuit; afraid that they would notice all the parts of me that really need to have the fat vacuumed out, or at least carpet-swept. But somehow I was not afraid to say it anymore. On that plane with all these beautiful young girls walking up the aisle as if it were a runway, if someone had exhibited so much as an angstrom of doubt about my beauty, I would have said that they could come kiss my big, beautiful, dimply, droopy butt.

However, as I said, this was before I got to the beach.

After unpacking in Huatulco, I put on my best black swimsuit. It was very expensive when I got it, very alluring. The only fly in the ointment was that it no longer fit. Actually, I'm not positive it ever did, but at least I used to be able to get it on without bruising. There in my room overlooking the turquoise sea, palm tree groves, and a sky of bright light blue, as I strained to pull the suit up past my thighs, I consoled myself by remembering that there is beauty in becoming so comfortable at being a mother, and a writer; there is grace in comfortableness. And of the several things of which I'm positive, one is that if I live to be an old woman, I won't be sitting on my porch berating myself for having leapt into a swimsuit to swim in warm ocean water at every opportunity even though my thighs were dimply. Also, most helpful of all, the wife of the couple we were traveling with—our best friends—has dimply thighs and a big butt too.

Maybe even bigger. Not that I'm comparing or anything.

Anyway. I got my suit on and waddled down to the beach.

I was not wearing a cover-up, not even a t-shirt. I had decided I was going to take my thighs and butt with me proudly wherever I went. I decided, in fact, on the way to the beach that I would treat them as if they were beloved elderly aunties, the kind who did embarrassing things at the beach, like roll their stockings into tubes around their ankles, but whom I was proud of because they were so great in every *real and important* way. So we walked along, the three of us, the aunties and I, to meet Sam and our friends in the sand. I imagined that I could feel the aunties beaming, as if they had been held captive in a dark closet too long, like Patty Hearst. Freed finally to stroll on a sandy Mexican beach: what a beautiful story.

It did not trouble me that parts of my body—the auntie parts—kept moving even after I had come to a full halt. Who cares? People just need to be soft and clean.

The first girls I saw were young, nine or ten, splashing around on the rocks near the shore, pretending to be horses. One of them was catching crabs. Iguanas watched with unblinking eyes from boulders that lined the walkway, and the three girls were fearless, unself-conscious and so lovely. At nine or ten, girls still get to be fine. They've still got a couple of years before they totally forget what they do have and start obsessing about what they don't. These girls had legs like baby egrets, probably not much changed from when they were seven or eight. They were still of an age when they could play without wearing the glasses of puberty that would make them see all their flaws. Not yet measuring, not yet comparing, still able to get caught up in crabs, in iguanas and currents, lost in what is right in front of them.

I was inspired. I found Sam and our friends on the beach, and we swam all afternoon, and everything was wonderful. Then I decided to head back up to my room for a little nap before dinner. Sam stayed with our friends on the beach. The aunties and I marched along in a way both strident and shy, until we got to one of the bus stops where the vans pick up people and drive them up the steep hillside. First I was alone, and that was nice, because I got to practice acting as if it were O.K. for a person with middle-aged thighs to stand around wearing only a swimsuit like other people. I smiled, thought fondly of the aunties, imaging one as Margaret Rutherford in old age, one as Samantha's dreamy aunt Clara in *Bewitched*, who could never get her spells to work.

And then out of nowhere, like dogs from hell, four teenage girls walked toward me to wait for the van.

They weren't wearing cover-ups either, but they were lovely and firm as models—I'd say that was the main difference—*and* all in bikinis. Two of them were already perfectly tan. And suddenly my trance was broken. Suddenly it was the Emperor's New Clothes, and I stood there in all of my fatitude like the tubby little emperor with his feta-cheese gut. In my mind now I looked like someone under fluorescent lights and felt in comparison to these girls like Roy Cohn in his last days. I wanted a trapdoor to open at my feet. And then—this is the truth—they *looked* at me. They looked at me standing there in the bright sunlight wearing only an ill-fitting swimsuit that had been laundered more times than the funds in Oliver North's campaign chest.

But then they made a fatal mistake. They looked at each other with these amused looks—the kind I must have given flabby women in swimsuits thirty years ago. And it gave me time to have two thoughts. One was not even a thought exactly: I just looked directly back at the four of them and heard the phantom clock playing in the background of their lives, "Tick, tock...tick, tock."

The other was the realization that I knew their secret: that they didn't think *they* were O.K. They were already in the hyper self-consciousness of the American teenage girl, and this meant that they were doomed. The smallest one probably thought she was too short, the other one too tall. The most beautiful one had no breasts, the buxom one had crisp thin hair.

My heart softened, and I could breathe again (although I would have killed for a sarong). I felt deep compassion for them; I wanted to tell them the good news—that at some point you give up on ever looking much better than you do. Somehow, you get a little older, a littler fatter, and you end up going a little easier on yourself. Or a lot easier. And I no longer felt ugly, maybe just a little ridiculous, I held my head a bit higher; I touched the aunties gently, to let them know I was there, and that made me less afraid. Ugliness is creeping around in fear, I remembered. Yet here I was, almost naked, and—to use the medical term—flabbier than shit, but deeply loyal to myself.

I forced myself not to check out their butts.

Finally, mercifully, a van came along and took us up the hill. The girls got off before me and walked toward their rooms. God—they had the most incredibly small butts. It made me want to kill myself.

When I got to my room, I took a long, hot shower and

then stood studying myself naked in the mirror. I looked like Divine. But then I thought about the poor aunties, how awful it must feel to have me judging them so harshly—the darling aunties! A gasp at this injustice escaped my lips, and my heart grew soft and maternal, and then I said out loud, "God! I am so sorry," and the aunties tucked their heads down shyly, not knowing now if they were safe. "Oh, *mon Dieu*," I told them and then, "Oh, my dears." I put on my sexiest t-shirt, my cutest underpants, and I slathered rose-scented lotion on my legs, rubbing it in gently with the indignation of a mother who has rescued her daughter from school-yard bullies or the hands of the Philistines.

I put on a little light foundation, as if making up a friend, a tiny bit of blusher, and way too much mascara—there are times when nothing else will do. Sam barged in, sunburned and hungry and demanding that we go to the dining room right that second, but the aunties and I ignored him.

Because now we were putting up our hair.

"Why do you have to do that when I'm *starving* to death?"

He wouldn't understand: he looks like a cross between God and Cindy Crawford. And I don't understand entirely either. But I knew to put on my favorite earrings. I wasn't thinking that I looked awful and wanted to look like someone else; that is the point at which you can come dangerously close to female impersonation. I just remembered that sometimes you start with the outside and you get it right. You tend to your spirit through the body. It's polishing the healthy young skin of that girl who was here just a moment ago, who still lives inside. It's saying that sometimes maybe one looks a little pale and wan and wants to shine a little light on oneself. Then, when you're in that honoring place, it's almost like makeup becomes a form of light, just as on those days when a little cloud cover makes you really notice the sun's rays that come slanting through. Maybe the key is simply a wry fondness for the thing you're slapping this stuff onto, instead of a desire to disguise; so it's not that you're wearing a coat of paint, but a mantilla.

*Anne Lamott is the author of many books, including the novels* Rosie, Crooked Little Heart, *and* Blue Shoe and Rosie. *Her nonfiction books include* Operating Instructions, Bird by Bird, Plan B: Further Thoughts on Faith, *and* Traveling Mercies: Some Thoughts on Faith, *from which this story was excerpted. She lives in Northern California.*

DAVID SEDARIS

# Jesus Shaves

*A French language class in Paris redefines the foundation of Christianity.*

"AND WHAT DOES ONE DO ON THE FOURTEENTH OF JULY? Does one celebrate Bastille Day?"

It was my second month of French class, and the teacher was leading us in an exercise designed to promote the use of "one," our latest personal pronoun.

"Might one sing on Bastille Day?" she asked. "Might one dance in the street? Somebody give me an answer."

Printed in our textbooks was a list of major holidays alongside a scattered arrangement of photos depicting French people in the act of celebration. The object was to match the holiday with the corresponding picture. It was simple enough but seemed an exercise better suited to the use of the word *they*. I didn't know about the rest of the class, but when Bastille Day eventually rolled around, I planned to stay home and clean my oven.

Normally, when working from the book, it was my habit to tune out my fellow students and scout ahead, concentrating on the question I'd calculated might fall to me, but this afternoon, we were veering from the usual format. Questions were answered on a volunteer basis, and I was able to sit back, confident that the same few students would do the talking. Today's discussion was dominated by an Italian nanny, two chatty Poles, and a pouty, plump Moroccan woman who had grown up speaking French and had enrolled in the class to improve her spelling. She'd covered these lessons back in the third grade and took every opportunity to demonstrate her superiority. A question would be asked and she'd give the answer, behaving as though this were a game show and, if quick enough, she might go home with a tropical vacation or a side-by-side refrigerator-freezer. By the end of her first day, she'd raised her hand so many times, her shoulder had given out. Now she just leaned back in her seat and shouted the answers, her bronzed arms folded across her chest like some great grammar genie.

I was doing my usual shuffle, trying to convey something in French to a horrified merchant, when my daughter Anna, then eight years old, took me aside and advised, "Daddy, you need a lot of spit in your mouth to speak French." Alas, my drooling has only caused more problems.

—James O'Reilly, "Troglodytes in Gaul"

We finished discussing Bastille Day, and the teacher moved on to Easter, which was represented in our textbook by a black-and-white photograph of a chocolate bell lying upon a bed of palm fronds.

"And what does one do on Easter? Would anyone like to tell us?" The Italian nanny was attempting to answer the question when the Moroccan student interrupted, shouting, "Excuse me, but what's an Easter?"

Despite her having grown up in a Muslim country, it seemed she might have heard it mentioned once or twice, but no. "I mean it," she said. "I have no idea what you people are talking about." The teacher then called upon the rest of us to explain.

The Poles led the charge to the best of their ability. "It is," said one, "a party for the little boy of God who call his self Jesus and...oh, shit."

She faltered, and her fellow countryman came to her aid.

"He call his self Jesus, and then he be die one day on two...morsels of...lumber."

The rest of the class jumped in, offering bits of information that would have given the pope an aneurysm. "He die one day, and then he go above of my head to live with your father."

"He weared the long hair, and after he died, the first day he come back here for to say hello to the peoples."

"He nice, the Jesus."

"He make the good things, and on the Easter we be sad because somebody makes him dead today."

Part of the problem had to do with grammar. Simple nouns such as cross and resurrection were beyond our grasp, let alone such complicated reflexive phrases as "To give of yourself your only begotten son." Faced with the challenge of explaining the cornerstone of Christianity, we did what any self-respecting group of people might do. We talked about food instead.

"Easter is a party for to eat of the lamb," the Italian nanny explained. "One, too, may eat of the chocolate."

"And who brings the chocolate?" the teacher asked.

I knew the word, and so I raised my hand, saying, "The Rabbit of Easter. He bring of the chocolate."

My classmates reacted as though I'd attributed the delivery to the Antichrist. They were mortified.

"A rabbit?" The teacher, assuming I'd used the wrong word, positioned her index fingers on top of her head, wiggling them as though they were ears. "You mean one of these? A rabbit rabbit?"

"Well, sure," I said. "He come in the night when one sleep on a bed. With a hand he have the basket and foods."

The teacher sadly shook her head, as if this explained everything that was wrong with my country. "No, no," she said. "Here in France the chocolate is brought by the big bell that flies in from Rome."

I called for a time-out. "But how do the bell know where you live?"

"Well," she said, "how does a rabbit?"

It was a decent point, but at least a rabbit has eyes. That's a start. Rabbits move from place to place, while most bells can only go back and forth—and they can't even do that on their own power. On top of that, the Easter Bunny has character; he's someone you'd like to meet and shake hands with. A bell has all the personality of a cast-iron skillet. It's like saying that come Christmas, a magic dustpan flies in from the North Pole, led by eight flying cinder blocks. Who wants to stay up all night so they can see a bell? And why fly one in from Rome when they've got more bells than they know what to do with right here in Paris? That's the most implausible aspect of the whole story, as there's no way the bells of France would allow a foreign worker to fly in and take their jobs. That Roman bell would be lucky to get work cleaning up after a French bell's dog—and even then he'd need papers. It just didn't add up.

Nothing we said was of any help to the Moroccan student. A dead man with long hair supposedly living with her father, a leg of lamb served with palm fronds and chocolate. Confused and disgusted, she shrugged her massive shoulders and turned her attention back to the comic book she kept hidden beneath her binder. I wondered then if, without the language barrier, my classmates and I could have done a better job making sense of Christianity, an idea that sounds pretty far-fetched to begin with.

In communicating any religious belief, the operative word is faith, a concept illustrated by our very presence in that classroom. Why bother struggling with the grammar lessons of a six-year-old if each of us didn't believe that, against all reason, we might eventually improve? If I could hope to one day carry on a fluent conversation, it was a relatively short leap to believing that a rabbit might visit my home in the middle of the night, leaving behind a handful of chocolate kisses and a carton of menthol cigarettes. So why stop there? If I could believe in myself, why not give other improbabilities the benefit of the doubt? I accepted the idea that an omniscient God had cast me in his own image and that he watched over me and guided me from one place to the next. The virgin birth, the resurrection, and the countless miracles—my heart expanded to encompass all the wonders and possibilities of the universe. A bell, though, that's fucked up.

*David Sedaris is a playwright, radio commentator, and author of several books including* Barrel Fever, Naked, *and* Me Talk Pretty One Day, *from which this story was excerpted. His most recent works include* SantaLand Diaries, Dress Your Family in Corduroy and Denim, *and* Children Playing Before a Statue of Hercules: An Anthology of Outstanding Stories. *He was named TIME*

*Magazine's Humorist of the Year in 2001, he received two Grammy nominations in 2005 for Best Spoken Word Album and Best Comedy Album, and his radio stories can be heard regularly on NPR's* This American Life.

Cartoon by Jack Ziegler

SOURAV SEN

# Benvenuto in Italia!

*It was time to surrender to the Gods of travel.*

ITALY WAS MY FIRST TASTE OF THE WORLD OUTSIDE INDIA. I was traveling from Delhi to meet my mother, who was traveling from Brussels. Our rendezvous was to be at Alitalia Gate 6, Terminal B, Aereoporto di Roma.

From Rome, we would travel together to Erice, the beautiful medieval town at the farthest tip of Sicily. There, Ma would attend a conference at Majorana Center, pronounced Mayorana, which will be later in this story. To get to Erice, one passes through Palermo, Italy's Mafia Capital.

A cheap Aeroflot flight brought me to Rome after a harrowing time and detention at the Moscow airport. The Russians had been convinced that my passport was forged. It was not. It was just that they could not imagine how, when my passport was European, my skin could be tan and my hair black. Their deduction was bolstered by the fact that I was traveling to Europe on a one-way ticket. To the Russian immigration officials, the truth could not be clearer: I was an illegal immigrant, with no intention to return to India! My passport was forged!

By the time the Russians finally cleared me for a flight to Rome, my baggage had been slashed open with a knife (you or I surely would have used the zipper instead) and every single sock had been turned inside out twice over by the determined customs agents. My freedom, when it finally came, cost me a pair of Levi's 501 and two cartons of Marlborough Lights. When I arrived in Rome, I was behind schedule and had neither slept a wink nor eaten a morsel in over forty hours. Worst of all, I had missed Ma at the airport. The neon sign in the arrival lounge flashed *Benvenuto in Italia!* Welcome to Italy!

My expectations of Italy had been built on the experience of friends. Chisti had been relieved of his black suitcase at the railway platform. He had even smiled back at the friendly young man who had walked by with his bright red suitcase. Only later did Chisti learn that the man's red luggage had been but a bottomless, molded plastic shell with a slit where the handle should have been. The artist (calling him a thief would be an insult to his creativity) had slipped the molded hollow over Chisti's luggage (obviously when my friend had been distracted), slipped the handle through the slit, and walked away with a red suitcase that was Chisti's, and black, a minute ago. Another friend, Manjeet, had been cheated of his money by uniformed (!) "policeman" demanding to examine his dollar bills "because of a crackdown on the import of counterfeit currency bills."

From the moment I stepped out of the plane in Rome, I regarded with suspicion everyone around me. Each person seemed to be staring strangely at me. Were they all harboring ownership ideas about my baggage? Were they wondering which planet I came from? With a three-day-old stubble on my sweat-stained face, unkempt hair, sleep-deprived eyelids, and my limp posture from carrying disfigured luggage, I must have raised many eyebrows. But, at that moment, I did not care how I looked. I just did not want to be noticed.

Now that I had missed Ma, and she had proceeded to Erice, I had to take a train to Palermo (a short-notice flight would have cost a fortune). I walked cautiously on along the platform, my arm wrapped around the bandaged baggage precariously balanced on my hip.

Suddenly, I noticed two men in Harley-Davidson jackets walking straight, and determinedly, at me. Uh-oh, I thought, freezing in my tracks for a moment. Then, I made a military-style about-face and quickened my pace without looking back. Like an ostrich, I believed that if I could not see them, they could not see me either.

Well, ostriches are not very smart creatures, and neither are people who think like ostriches do. The two men overtook me and stopped me in my path. One of them retrieved his picture ID from inside his jacket and thrust it at my face. It was a picture ID for sure, but there was no way of knowing if it was a military pass or just a library card.

Then, the heavier-built of the two spewed a minute or two of pure Italian on my grimy face. To me, it was all Greek. I was speechless as my mind raced through if-then scenarios. I could hear Chisti saying "Itoldya," and I could see the Russian airport authorities' smirking faces. I could see Ma waiting endlessly for me at the Majorana Center, and I could see myself homeless, penniless in Rome. I had to think fast. I settled for the classic "dunno whatchya sayin" approach.

That's exactly what I said to them, in Hindi, which, I was sure they would not understand. "*Kya keh rahe ho, patha nahin, mujhe kuchh samajh nahin aata, mujhe aapki bhashaa nahie aati, mere paas kuchh nahi hai, jaane doe....*" I rattled off endlessly.

For some reason, I hoped that their inability to comprehend what I was saying would discourage them from bothering me further. I was wrong. A heavy, vice-like grip landed on my shoulder as one of them announced "la Polizia" in the most authoritative voice I had heard since Moscow.

This time, there was no doubt about what they meant, and it kindled an image of Manjeet without his dollars. However, there was no escape. Or so I thought—at first. Then, I swiftly ducked to loosen the vice on my shoulder, did a figure-skating spin, and darted in the opposite direction like a cheetah.

But there really was no escape. I ran into a woman in a police uniform, waiting with arms akimbo for me. Actually, I was glad to see a police officer in uniform—quite a contrast to the impostors in denims. Although Manjeet had warned me about uniform-wearing "police," I put my faith in this lady, explaining to her why I was running. I asked that she arrest the two thugs immediately.

But as it turned out, the thugs were indeed genuine policemen. "At least, my money is safe," I sighed in relief as the muscles around my wallet relaxed. I reasoned that I had been under suspicion because of my ragged looks and my self-conscious gait. I could explain, I told Signora Poliziotta, in response to her stare. Sure, she seemed to say, but she wanted to see my passport.

Passport! Not again. I would have given anything to avoid a replay of the Russian drama in Italian. I was determined to discourage her about the passport. For some reason, I thought I might succeed because I looked somewhat Italian. And I seemed to make some headway with my politeness and smile, as I skillfully steered the focus of the conversation. That was until she asked me where I was going.

Strange is an understatement for how the mind works.

Amnesia struck me just then! Where *was* I going? I had to say something to save my life. Something. *Anything*. But I could not lie. Not to the police. I had to answer, and pronto.

"Mafia town," I stammered. "Mafia town?" she questioned, raising her eyebrows.

I knew that I should have done better—but it was too late. Suddenly the name of the town flashed in my mind.

"Palermo!" I yelled with joy.

"Palermo?" the cynical tone of one of the policemen behind me reminded me that I had more people than just this lady to charm.

"Actually, I will proceed from there," I volunteered, turning to face the two policemen in leather jackets, "to the Marijuana Center…."

I felt the familiar vice-grip on my shoulder once again.

*Benvenuto in Italia!*

*Sourav Sen has lived in Delhi, India and Innsbruck, Austria, and now lives in Oakland, California. He was trained as an architect, a planner, and a pilot. By daylight, he works as an investment analyst in San Francisco; by moonlight, he is a freelance writer.*

GERMAINE W. SHAMES

# Mexican Mating Calls

*The author raises the eternal question: Is love amphibious?*

ONCE I HAD A LOVER—LET'S CALL HIM JUAN—WHOSE English was, at best, rudimentary. But Juan spoke the universal language like a master. On his silvery tongue, even the most garbled expressions took my breath away.

Juan and I met in Mexico, his country of birth, my temporary residence. Land of the *piropo* (verbal tributes to feminine charms), of long songs and laments, Mexico was the perfect setting for a storybook romance, and Juan, as I said, was well-suited to the role of Don Juan.

"My love, my heart, my life," he'd croon, looking deep into my eyes with a fiery gaze that made my heart smolder, "I love you with every breath I take, I can't live without you. You are the queen of my existence, and I your slave."

Whether or not I believed Juan, I can't really say. So dazzled was I by his declarations of love, so mesmerized by the burning look that accompanied them, discernment failed me. Juan made me feel desired, cherished, worshipped. His words entered my bloodstream like an elixir and made my heart *cha-cha-cha*. In love with Juan's verbiage, I let it work its magic and asked no questions.

Life with Juan was all-day siestas and all night fiestas, serenades at my balcony, roses at my doorstep, and Juan pinned to my ear, cooing his inimitable Mexican mating calls.

"My nightingale, my heaven, my saint," he'd tell me, letting the words trickle down my earlobe like warm honey. "I love you with every beat of my heart. You're part of my very being, as essential as the air I breathe. If you left me, I swear I would die."

Leave Juan? I supposed I might one day, but I was in no hurry. Life as Juan's *novia* (sweetheart) was sweet indeed. As long as the nectar in Juan's tongue continued to flow, I saw no reason for our idyll to end. Latin courtships might last months, years, long enough for me to soak up volumes of Juan's odes and oaths.

"My light, my soul, my treasure," he'd whisper endlessly, growing bolder, drawing me closer, so close I could see the facets in his eyes glow like hot coals. "I love you more than I love myself, more that your own mother loves you, more than—may the Virgin forgive me!—more than God Himself could ever love you. I swear I would die for you."

Fortunately for most Juans, few loves are ever actually put to the test. No doubt, my Juan banked on not having to make good on his claims. He was only telling me what I wanted to hear, after all: words of love.

But, as fate would have it, circumstances intervened—drastic circumstances—that thrust my very life into his hands.

One weekend Juan took me to a small seaside resort outside Playa Blanca where we intended to spend a few quiet days romancing to the rhythm of the waves. The setting—white-hot sands, placid sea, a caressing breeze—had all the promise of a sultry summer daydream. Shortly after our arrival, however, a nasty storm blew in, and the tide rose like a waterfall in reverse.

For two days Juan and I kept to our sweltering hotel room, glued together by our own perspiration. Whatever the mosquitoes spared of me, Juan nibbled at unceasingly, until every pore of my body stung. By day three—the last of our little holiday—raw, dehydrated, half-incinerated, I decided to have a swim come what may.

Out I ran to the beach with Juan calling after me, "My love, the sea she's mean. Don't go!"

He was right. I was no match for the waves, and they had their way with me. Tossed about like a dummy, suctioned down into the drink again and again, I quickly felt my fight give out. I was drowning.

"Help me, Juan!" I screamed. My mouth filled with brine each time I opened it. "Help me! Help! Help...!"

"Sweem, *mamacita*, sweem!" Juan cried back.

"Help!" I cried desperately, a dozen times, a hundred, though Juan had no doubt heard me the first time.

"Sweem, *por Dios* (for God's sake)! Sweem!" he repeated, matching me yelp for yelp.

The poor man was beside himself, clearly. He ran up and down the beach, weeping, wailing; he tore his hair, waved his arms, fell to his knees...and never so much as wet the tips of his toes.

When a wayward wave finally heaved me onto the beach where he waited dry and safe, I couldn't help but feel sorry for him. Not meaning to, I had exposed him; his words had been so much flotsam.

But Juan showed no signs of embarrassment. To the contrary, his face lit up and he shed tears of joy.

"My goddess, my angel, my adoration...." he cooed, riveting me once more with his searing gaze as he led me away.

*Germaine W. Shames is author of the critically acclaimed novel,* Between Two Deserts. *She has written from six continents—soon to add the seventh—on topics ranging from the Middle East crisis to the plight of street children. Her essays and short fiction have been widely anthologized; her articles appear in such periodicals as* National Geographic Traveler, Hemispheres, *and* Success. *She was last spotted piloting a narrow boat up the Grand Union Canal, accompanied by an Anglicized gorilla.*

BILL BRYSON

* * *

# What's Cooking?

*It's not so simple anymore.*

GOING TO A RESTAURANT IS GENERALLY A DISCOURAGING experience for me because I always manage somehow to antagonize the waitress. This, of course, is something you never want to do because waitresses are among the relatively small group of people who have the opportunity to sabotage items that you will shortly be putting in your mouth.

My particular problem is being unable to take in all the food options that are presented to me. If you order, say, a salad, the waitress reels off sixteen dressings, and I am not quick enough to take in that many concepts at once.

"Can you run those past me again?" I say with a simpleton smile of the sort that I hope will inspire compassion.

So the waitress sighs lightly and rolls her eyes a trifle, the way you would if you had to recite sixteen salad dressings over and over all day long for a succession of half-wits, and reels off the list again. This time I listen with the greatest gravity and attentiveness, nodding at each, and then unfailingly I choose one that she didn't mention.

"We don't do Thousand Island," she says flatly.

I can't possibly ask her to recite the list again, so I ask for the only one I can remember, which I am able to remember only because it sounded so awful—Gruyère and goat's milk vinaigrette or something. Lately I have hit on the expedient of saying: "I'll have whichever one is pink and doesn't smell like the bottom of a gym bag." They can usually relate to that, I find.

In fancy restaurants it is even worse because the server has to take you through the evening's specials, which are described with a sumptuousness and panache that are seldom less than breathtaking and always incomprehensible. My wife and I went to a fancy restaurant in Vermont for our anniversary the other week and I swear I didn't understand a single thing the waiter described to us.

"Tonight," he began with enthusiasm, "we have a crepe *galette* of sea chortle and kelp in a rich *mal de mer* sauce, seasoned with disheveled herbs grown in our own herbarium. This is baked in an inverted Prussian helmet for seventeen minutes and four seconds precisely, then layered with steamed wattle and *woozle* leaves. Very delicious; very audacious. We are also offering this evening a double rack of Rio Ròcho cutlets, tenderized at your table by our own flamenco dancers, then baked in a clay *dong* for twenty-seven minutes under a lattice of guava peel and sun-ripened stucco. For vegetarians this evening we have a medley of forest floor sweetmeats gathered from our very own woodland dell...."

And so it goes for anything up to half an hour. My wife, who is more sophisticated than I, is not fazed by the ornate terminology. Her problem is trying to keep straight the bewilderment of options. She will listen carefully, then say;

I'm sorry, is it the squib that's pan-seared and presented on a bed of organic *spoletto*?"

"No, that's the baked *donkling*," says the serving person. "The squib comes as a quarter-cut hank, lightly rolled in *payapaya*, then tossed with oil of *olay* and calamine, and presented on a bed of chaff beans and *snoose* noodles."

I don't know why she bothers because, apart from being much too complicated to take in, none of the dishes sounds like anything you would want to eat anyway, except maybe on a bet after drinking way too much.

Now all this is of particular moment to me because I have just been reading the excellent *Diversity of Life* by the eminent Harvard naturalist Edward O. Wilson, in which he makes the startling and discordant assertion that the foods we in the Western world eat actually are not very adventurous at all.

Wilson notes that of the 30,000 species of edible plants on earth, only about 20 are eaten in any quantity. Of these, 3 species alone—wheat, corn, and rice—account for over half of what the temperate world shovels into its collective gullet. Of the 3,000 fruits known to botany, all but about 2 dozen are essentially ignored. The situation with vegetables is a little better, but only a little.

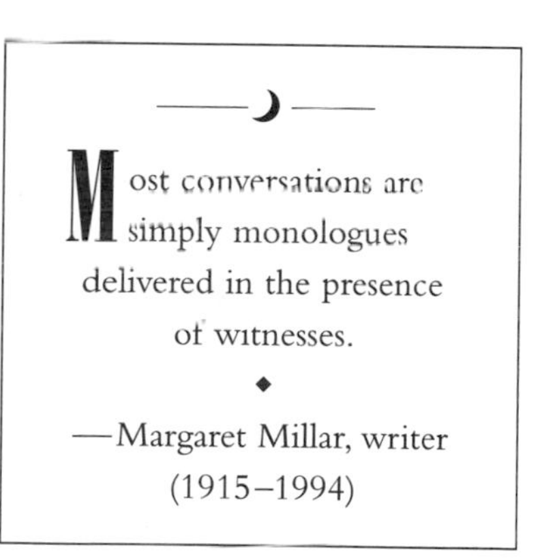

Most conversations are simply monologues delivered in the presence of witnesses.

—Margaret Millar, writer (1915–1994)

And why do we eat the few meager foods we do? Because, according to Wilson, those were the foods that were cultivated by our Neolithic ancestors 10,000 or so years ago when they first got the hang of agriculture.

The very same is true of husbandry. The animals we raise for food today are not eaten because they are especially nutritious or delectable but because they were the ones first domesticated in the Stone Age.

In other words, in dietary terms we are veritable troglodytes (which, speaking personally, is all right by me). I think this explains a lot, not least my expanding sense of dismay as the waiter bombarded us with ecstatic descriptions of roulades, ratatouilles, empanadas, langostinos, *tagliolinis*, confits, phyllos, quenelles, and goodness knows what else.

"Just bring me something that's been clubbed," I wanted to say, but of course I held my tongue.

Eventually, he concluded his presentation with what sounded to me like "an oven-baked *futilité* of pumpkin rind and kumquats."

"It's *feuilleté*," my wife explained to me.

"And what's that when you take it out of the box?" I asked unhappily.

"Something you wouldn't like, dear."

I turned to the waiter with a plaintive look. "Do you have anything that once belonged to a cow?" I asked.

He gave a stiff nod. "Certainly, sir. We can offer you a sixteen-ounce *suprême de boeuf*, incised by our own butcher from the foreflank of a corn-fed Holstein raised on our own Montana ranch, then slow-grilled over palmetto and buffalo chips at the temperature of..."

"Are you describing a steak?" I asked, perking up.

"Not a term we care to use, sir, but yes."

Of course. It was all becoming clear now. There was real food to be had here if you just knew the lingo. "Well, I'll have that," I said. "And I'll have it with, shall we say, a *dépravaté* of potatoes, hand cut and fried till golden in a medley of vegetable oils from the Imperial Valley, accompanied by a *quantité de bière*, flash-chilled in your own coolers and conveyed to my table in a cylinder of glass."

The man nodded, impressed that I had cracked the code. "Very good, sir," he said. He clicked his heels and withdrew.

"And no *feuilleté*," I called after him. I may not know much about food, but I am certain of this: If there is one thing you don't want with steak it's *feuilleté*.

*Bill Bryson was born in Des Moines, Iowa. For twenty years he lived in England, where he worked for the* Times *and the* Independent. *His books include travel memoirs (*Neither Here Nor There, The Lost Continent, Notes from a Small Island, A Walk in the Woods, In a Sunburned Country*), books on language (*The Mother Tongue, Made in America*) and the more recent works,* Bill Bryson's African Diary *and* A Short History of Nearly Everything. *This story was excerpted from* I'm a Stranger Here Myself: Notes on Returning to America after Twenty Years Away. *In 2003, after eight years in the U.S., he returned to England, where he lives with his wife and their four children.*

NIGEL BARLEY

# The Dentist in Cameroon

*An anthropologist with a toothache experiences a case of mistaken identity.*

FINALLY I ARRIVED AT GAROUA WHERE, I HAD BEEN INformed, there lurked a dentist, the only other one in Cameroon being in the capital. After many red herrings involving putative Red Chinese dentists who turned out to be tractor drivers, I eventually tracked the man down at the local hospital.

Being still at the stage of the Western woolly-minded liberal, I took my place in the queue and waited. After some time, a French businessman arrived. He shouldered his way to the front of the queue and gave the nurse 500 francs. "Is there a white dentist?" he asked. The nurse demurred, "He's not white but he's from France." The expatriate considered this and left. I stayed.

As soon as the surgery door opened, I found myself propelled by waiting Africans to the front of the queue. Within was a certain amount of dilapidated dental equipment and a large diploma from the University of Lyons, which reassured me somewhat. I explained the problem to a huge man inside.

Without more ado, he seized a pair of pliers and pulled out my two front teeth. The unexpectedness of the attack somewhat dulled my sense to the pain of the extraction. The teeth, he declared, were rotten. He had removed them. I was cured. I should pay the nurse outside. I sat blankly in the chair, blood gushing down my shirtfront, and tried to make him understand that he could now proceed to the next stage of his treatment. It is not easy to argue in a foreign tongue in the absence of two front teeth; I made little progress. Finally, he understood that I was a difficult patient. Very well, he declared huffily, if I was not content with his treatment, he would bring the dentist himself. He disappeared, leaving me wondering who had just operated upon me. I had fallen into the obvious trap of believing that anyone in a dental surgery, wearing a white coat and prepared to extract teeth, was a dentist.

Another man appeared, also in a white coat. Swiftly, I asked whether he was the dentist. He agreed that he was. This other man was his mechanic; he also repaired watches. A dental repair to bridge the hole in my apparatus would be very expensive. It was very difficult and required great skill. He had that skill. I tried to explain to him that unless I could talk, I could not work. If I could not work, I could not pay him. He brightened visibly. I should return in the afternoon. He would confect a plastic device. As a valued patient, I qualified for an anesthetic. He injected Novocain into my gums. It seemed a strange thing to do after the operation, but I felt too wretched to care.

I spent a somewhat awkward interval wandering around Garoua, gap-toothed and werewolf-fanged. People approaching me crossed the street to avoid passing too close. There was so much blood on my chest that I looked as if I had been mortally wounded. I could only lisp and stutter explanations to inquisitive gendarmes who clearly suspected me of some vile act of human dismemberment.

In the afternoon I returned and received two plastic teeth that balanced precariously on my gums and a bottle of pink liquid to gargle with. I was charged ten times the legal rate for treatment but knew no better than to pay up. As I left, I noticed the syringe I had been injected with lying on the floor.

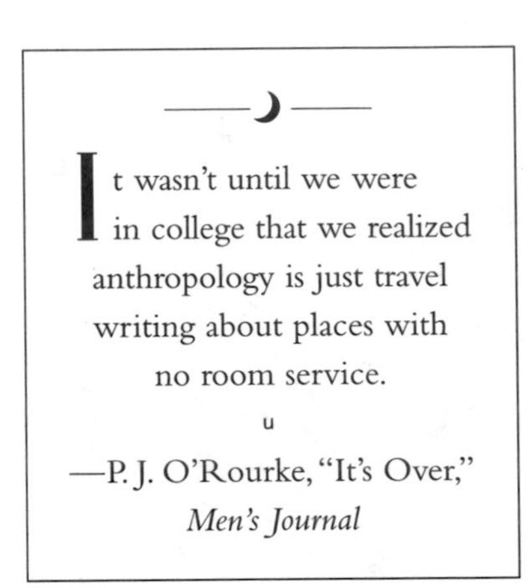

It wasn't until we were in college that we realized anthropology is just travel writing about places with no room service.

—P. J. O'Rourke, "It's Over," *Men's Journal*

Learning to cope with this dreadful prosthetic device was a complication I could well have done without. The Dowayos (the tribe I was living with), of course, were delighted with it: many of them have their front teeth filed away to resemble my condition. I asked them why they did this? Was it for beauty? Oh no. Was it—and here the anthropologist was indulging his fancy—to provide for the body an entrance which was the same shape as the gate at the entrance to the village? Oh no, *patron*. They did it, they informed me, so that if a man's jaw locked solid, they could still push food into his mouth and he could eat. Did this happen often? As far as anyone knew it had never happened, but it might. My ability to remove my teeth, and even more, their own ability and willingness to remove themselves in midconversation, were matters of great interest to Dowayos.

*Nigel Barley was senior anthropologist for the British Museum until 2003. He spent several years living in Cameroon, and in 2002 won the Foreign Press Association Prize for Travel. His books include* Not a Hazardous Sport, Ceremony: An Anthropologist's Misadventures in the African Bush, *and* The Innocent Anthropologist: Notes from a Mud Hut, *from which this story was excerpted.*

*

When Oyewale Tomori went to lunch in New Haven, the counter man noticed something strange about his customer. He spoke a lilting English, possibly Caribbean in origin, and he consumed his submarine sandwich with tremendous gusto.

"Where are you from?" asked the man.

"The Yale Arbovirus Research Unit," said Tomori.

"I mean, where are you *from*?"

"I'm from Nigeria."

"You're from Africa!"

"Yes, I told you, I'm from Nigeria."

"I've watched a lot of films about Africa. Do you know Tarzan?"

"Sure I know Tarzan," said Tomori. "We're good friends."

There was a pause before the next question. "Is it true they hunt heads and eat people in Africa?"

"Yes, it's true. But heads are very difficult to come by now. So we're sending people out to search for heads in other parts of the world. In fact, I'm here in New Haven hunting for heads."

—Thomas A. Bass, *Camping with the Prince and Other Tales of Science in Africa*

WILLIAM DALRYMPLE

# The Crafty Cousin

*He thinks as fast as he drives.*

THE TAXI DRIVER WHO TOOK ME BACK FROM THE SYRIAN Orthodox cathedral told me this story as we crawled through the bazaars behind an ambling train of pack mules:

"My cousin is a taxi driver in Damascus. One day he was waiting by some traffic lights when a limousine with clouded glass window smashed into his rear. The back of the taxi was completely wrecked. My cousin is a hot-blooded man—we all are in my family—so he jumped out and began to harangue the occupants, calling them sons of unmarried mothers, brothers of incontinent camels, fathers of she-goats and so on. After two minutes of this, the rear window of the limousine lowered half an inch, and a visiting card was thrust through the crack. On it was written a single telephone number. My cousin started shouting, 'What is the meaning of this?' but the window was wound up again and the limousine swerved around him and his concertina-ed taxi, leaving him shouting into space.

"My cousin was determined to get some compensation from the rich man who owned the car, so the following day he went to a phone box and rang the number that had been written on the card. He started by softening the man up with a few pleasantries, then went on to demand a new taxi, saying that fifteen people depended on the money he brought home, that his wife was sick and that his daughter was getting married the following year.

"There was no response to this, so my cousin began to get angry again, comparing the man to the vomit of an Israeli dog and the worms which wriggle in the belly of a wild pig. He had been speaking like this for five minutes when suddenly a quiet voice on the end of the line said: 'Do you have any idea who you are talking to?'

"'No,' replied my cousin.

"'You are speaking to Hafez al-Assad,' said a sinister voice. 'As you may be aware, I am the President of the Syrian Arab Republic.'

"'I know who you are,' said my cousin without hesitation, 'but do you have any idea who *you* are talking to?'

"'No,' said the voice, surprised.

"'Thank God for that,' said my cousin, slamming down the phone and running to his car as fast as he could, before the *mukhabarat* could trace the call and treat him to an extended stay at President Assad's pleasure."

*William Dalrymple wrote the highly acclaimed bestseller* In Xanadu *when he was twenty-two. His second book,* City of Djinns, *won the 1994 Thomas Cook Travel Book Award and the Sunday Times Young British Writer of the Year Award. His contributions to British popular understanding of culture and history have included numerous television series and radio shows. He divides his time among London, Edinburgh, and Delhi where he lives with his wife and three children. This story was excerpted from his book,* From the Holy Mountain: A Journey Among the Christians of the Middle East.

*

"You are Martik Bargarian, Armenian sausage merchant," Reza announced, dangling a hotel key at me.

"What?"

The room apparently was four dollars, but would be fifty if the hotel manager suspected I was a foreigner.

"So you just talk sausage. O.K.?"

Muttering in a stilted guttural drawl about sausages, I was virtually carried through the lobby between Reza and Ghossam. We had one room with six single cots in it. The bathroom was truly terrifying, a bat cave with faucets.

After listening to the duet for tuba and whoopee cushion that emerged from my companions' noses and mouths all night, I felt sure I had not slept even half a wink by the time an iridescent gray sheen appeared beyond the begrimed glass veil of our curtainless windows.

—Paul William Roberts, *In Search of the Birth of Jesus: The Real Journey of the Magi*

**Pushing the limits of consumer-rights activism**

LUIS ALBERTO URREA

# Incident at San Antonio

*Here's proof that men are the bosses.*

THERE ISN'T MUCH TO THE VILLAGE OF SAN ANTONIO.

It is easy to drive past it, thinking there is nothing there but a roadside soda stand. It's a tiny hamlet on a bend in the road in an area of vineyards. There are a couple of houses and two stores, side by side. Near the stores you will see a whitewashed adobe wall with a large gate in it and a sign that says, Estado 29. It is an orphanage, State Orphanage Number Twenty-nine.

I was taking one of the boys from Twenty-nine to the store; we had to buy some lard for the cook, and I was going to get him a lollipop and a Coke.

Along the side of one of the stores is a wooden bench. Unemployed men sit here all day and drink beer. (It has always seemed a miracle to me that Mexican men, without one cent, produce enough money to get thoroughly drunk.) When we are in the area, working, they stare at us, not sure what to do about it. They clearly think they ought to be heckling us, at the very least. On this day they were busy arguing drunkenly, waggling fingers at each other and standing up to make pronouncements, then sitting back down and crossing their arms with a flourish, like characters out of *Tortilla Flat*.

Suddenly, the door of the house behind the store slammed, and a woman in tight Levi's and a knit sweater appeared in the street. She stood there, glaring at the men.

One of them in particular was apparently the focus of her gaze. He tipped down the bill of his cap, trying to be invisible. That didn't work. He huffed and straightened up and flung his arms out as if exasperated by her nagging. "What do you want?" he sneered, in a ploy obviously intended more for his compadres than for her.

They looked quite pleased with him.

She said nothing.

Emboldened, he said, "Answer me!"

Silent, she pulled a set of car keys out of her pocket and held them up for him to see.

He stood.

"Give me those keys!" he ordered

She turned on her heel and walked away.

"Don't you *ever*," he announced, finger pointing, "walk away from me!"

The drunks were stirring.

She was heading for a car.

"Don't touch that car!"

She touched it: she opened the door.

"I'm telling you to get away from that car!" He took a wobbly step toward her.

The compadres were impressed with him, that much was obvious.

"And don't think you're getting inside!"

She got in.

The drunks were mortified.

"*¡Hija de puta!*" he squealed. "I'll kill you! *[¡Te mato!]* Do *not* start that %#$@!*! engine!"

She started the engine and popped it in gear.

He was bright crimson by now.

In slow, threatening cadence, he warned, "Don't. You. DARE. Drive. Away. IN MY CAR!"

She peeled out, splattering him with dirt and pebbles.

The drunks hung their heads, looked away.

We all watched her speed off toward Ensenada. She never slowed own. When the car was a mere wink in the distance, he drew himself up to full height and shouted, "All right! Fine! But don't even *think* about bringing the car back!"

The compadres were delighted.

"You told her!" they cried, slapping his back, opening more beers.

He reclaimed his seat among them and smiled.

"The man," he said, sighing, "is always on top. That's just the way it is."

*Luis Alberto Urrea was born in Tijuana to an American mother and a Mexican father. He graduated from the University of California, did relief work on the Mexican border, and later taught expository writing at Harvard. His first book,* Across the Wire: Life and Hard Times on the Mexican Border, *was a New York Times Notable Book of the Year. Luis currently resides in Chicago and teaches at the University of Illinois. He has three kidlets and is happily married to Cinderella. The family can often be found driving across America in a brown van blaring Goth rock, techno, and latino music. If there is such a thing as reincarnation, he wants to come back as Emiliano Zapata. This story was excerpted from* By the Lake of Sleeping Children: The Secret Life of the Mexican Border.

*

Inside, a man sprawled languidly across several burlap sacks, smoking a water pipe and grinning, like a fat Cheshire cat.

"I am Mohammed, at your service," he said, straightening his turban. "You want change money? You want sugar?" He paused. "You want bayonet?"

I smiled noncommittally. He opened a drawer. "These just in from Iran," he said, dropping a plump green grenade in my hand. "For you I make a special deal. Other villages, you find grenades only at Friday market. At Mohammed's every day."

At this point I half expected him to hand me a promotional flier. Free Bayonet with Every Sack of Sugar! Grenades Every Day! These Just in from Iran! I changed twenty dollars at a favorable rate, climbed back in the car, and headed deeper into the hills.

—Tony Horwitz, *Baghdad Without a Map, and Other Misadventures in Arabia*

RANDY WAYNE WHITE

# A Train, a Frog, and Aliens

*...all meet at the power vortices of Sedona, Arizona.*

ITEM IN AMTRAK'S *EXPRESS MAGAZINE*: NEARLY EVERY forty-eight hours, motorist impatience or inattention causes a vehicle collision with an Amtrak train. On board, Amtrak passengers seldom feel more than a bump. But it can be far more serious for the motorist.

I find the above interesting because after a day aboard Amtrak's transcontinental passenger train, the *Sunset Limited*, I have noticed more than a few bumps. Nothing uncomfortable. Just the occasional ka-THUMP inserted into the lulling and steady humpity-humpity-humpity-humpity of the diesel engine spiriting us across the nation. Sealed within my deluxe sleeper, even the riverboat wail of the train's whistle is hushed, so the unexpected ka-THUMPS are felt more than heard; staccato jolts that interrupt the metronomic swaying of the train.

After reading *Express Magazine*, I begin to wonder what kind of automotive debris we might be dragging beneath us. After all, it has been nearly ten hours since I boarded in

Winter Haven, Florida, bound for Los Angeles. Statistically, we've had a fair shot at intersecting with a Toyota or two, or perhaps a souped-up Chevy run amok at some country crossing. As I consider the possibilities, Mr. Graham, the attendant, taps at my cabin door. After he takes my dinner reservation, I ask him if, in his thirteen years on the job, he has ever been aboard a train that hit a car. Mr. Graham does not hesitate. "Oh, yes sir, many times, sir. But it's nothing you need to worry about. We don't feel much of anything up here." Up here meaning the upper deck of a superliner car where everything—observation car, dining car, my sleeper—is elevated fifteen feet above the earth.

So it was possible that we had already hit a car?

"Not this trip. You'll know if we hit a car because we got to sit around while the wrecker hauls the thing off the track. Then we got to call the attorneys. Just getting the coroner out takes two, three hours sometimes." Mr. Graham's expression shares with me the frustrations of trying to maintain a railroad schedule in an unappreciative, unpredictable jet age America.

Because I enjoy riding trains, I am empathetic. "Yeah, those coroners. It all pays the same to them."

When I am not chatting with Mr. Graham, and when I am not in the dining car joking with the waiters, or when I am not in the observation car meeting fellow passengers, I join my traveling companion in our cabin where I watch the American South roll by. Thus far, the American South has consisted of whistle stops at Kissimmee, Orlando, Palatka, Tallahassee, and a dozen other Florida towns, most of it Magic Kingdom tourist sprawl and orange grove country. The stops inspire little comment from me, and none from my companion. I have seen it before, for I am a Floridian, and my companion is indifferent, because he is a frog—a southern bullfrog, to be precise; a fully grown saddle back, as the old time giggers in the Everglades call large frogs, and I am taking him to California to compete in a famous jumping frog contest.

But that is another story.

For now we are riding the westbound *Sunset Limited*, routed through Alabama, Mississippi, Louisiana, Texas, then along the Mexican border into New Mexico, Arizona, and California. We are on the port side of car 130, room E, a cabin as practical and efficient as the cabin of a good boat. There is a sink, a hose shower in the head, a bunk above, and a settee that pulls out into a bed. The outboard wall is nearly six feet of double thick Margard Glass, so I spend most of my time in the chair by the window, reading and watching the countryside roll by. The frog, along with a dozen live crickets, stays in a Tupperware box, where I hope all of them will remain for the duration of this three-day trip. The Amtrak literature does not mince words when it comes to pets. They are "expressly prohibited," and, while it could be argued that a bullfrog is not a pet, it has always been my philosophy that it is easier to apologize than it is to ask permission.

So we sit in our cabin, a quiet cell in a honeycomb of sleepers. Our car is the last of ten cars, all linked to a pair of robotic-looking locomotives—the overall effect of which is to feel a part of some elemental force that displaces great volumes of air as the landscape slides past.

From this elevated vantage point, the mundane, the less mobile, the clotted car traffic, and the stranded townspeople, all seem as temporal, or as trivial, as just another bump on the tracks.

*

Not counting the frog, there are more than three hundred passengers aboard this train; seats are booked months in advance, so we were very lucky to get a Deluxe Sleeper, though I would have settled for a Family Sleeper, or even an Economy Sleeper. What I didn't want was to spend three nights in a reclining coach seat, shoulder to elbow with a bunch of strangers who, I feared, would demonstrate as little sympathy for my life-long insomnolence as my choice of traveling companions. I know from experience that, by day, the cost of a sleeper seems extravagant but, come 3 A.M., it is the last nickel bargain in town. In the dining car last night, I was seated with Mark and Anne of Clearwater, Florida, an attractive, athletic couple who have taken a break in their routine of jogging, cycling, and all-around healthy living to travel by coach car to New Orleans. This morning when I saw them at breakfast, though, they hardly seemed to be the same people. They appeared gaunt, unsteady, and bleary eyed, as if haunted by the coronas of lights.

"It was hellish," Mark said, describing the night he and his wife had spent. "We were right by the door. It kept opening and closing, opening and closing. I hate that door! I tried to drink myself to sleep, but even that didn't work."

Anne told me, "When we get to our hotel in New Orleans, it's straight to bed."

I said very little. They seemed too frail to endure gloating, and I had had a great night. After a steak dinner, I decided to forgo the movie in the observation coach (a car walled and roofed with windows) as well as bingo in the club car. Instead, I returned to my sleeper, fed the frog, then showered. There was a bucket of ice thoughtfully stocked by Mr. Graham, so I dug out a can of beer and sat with lights off, by the window. The observation car is fine by day; a fun place to eavesdrop and meet fellow travelers, but nightfall is a more intimate time, particularly on a train, and I wanted to enjoy it alone. There was no moon, so the few vignettes of landscape visible were isolated and set apart by the darkness: the arc of a basketball on a deserted playground; a woman framed by a lighted window, stretching to brush her hair; the truck stop haze of the cities and small towns, Pensacola and Myrtle Grove; the deep south gloom of pine forest that, by darkening my window, allowed previous images to linger for a time, flickering and fading like dying fires. Traveling at night by train, the sense of motion and the sense of time are transposed, so there is a growing illusion that you are a stationary observer of those who exist beyond the window—and their lives are speeding past at a terrible velocity.

I slept well. A train may be the best place in the world to sleep, because movement is the lone antidote for a restless spirit. The only interruption I had was after I switched on a light to read, and Mr. Graham tapped at the door and poked his head in. "You need an extra blanket? More ice?"

I told him I was fine.

The attendant paused for a moment, his expression slowly describing puzzlement. "Say," he said finally, "do you hear that? Sounds like...crickets."

In the frog's box, the crickets were singing their death song—but I couldn't tell Mr. Graham about that.

I nodded toward the window. "I think we must be passing a swamp."

Mr. Graham considered that for a moment, unconvinced. Then he said, "That's right, that's right, we are. Be due to cross the river into Mobile pretty soon. The crickets are out tonight!"

*

People who are devoted to physical integrity and personal fitness may find the sedentary life aboard a train irksome—even I was beginning to feel a little stodgy. So when it was announced that we would have a two-hour layover in New Orleans, I put on shorts and running shoes and jogged out of Union Terminal, past the Superdome, toward the French Quarter. But running at midday in New Orleans is not easy. The air is as heavy as hot silk, and every block is spiced with the odor of a different restaurant, each a temptation. After about ten minutes of intensive exercise, I decided I had earned a light meal so, on St. Charles Street, I stepped into the Pearl Restaurant, a working-class bistro with linoleum floors, high ceiling fans, and a lunch counter. Chuck was working behind the bar, and he recommended oysters. I had a dozen, raw. Chuck observed that it was a shame I didn't have time to try the fried oysters, because they were very good, too. I did have time, so I had a dozen of those, plus a bottle of local beer, Dixie Amber Light. I sat there eating and talking with Chuck (people at The Pearl were wonderfully chatty—uncommon in busy, big city restaurants) so I chose to prolong my stay by ordering a plate of red beans. Chuck served the beans smoking hot, with cornbread and a thick cut of sausage, and he placed another iced bottle of beer on the counter. After the beans, I was trying to choose between an order of seafood gumbo or Miss Leola's jambalaya when Chuck mentioned that they had just taken a bucket of Cajun boiled potatoes from the cooler, and would I like to try a couple on the house?

I was midway through my second potato, still conversing with Chuck, when I happened to notice that the clock on the wall didn't match the watch on my wrist. To my horror, I realized that last night I had mistakenly backed my watch two hours, not one, when adjusting for the time zone change—instead of having more than an hour to get back to the train, I had less than ten minutes. With the barest of explanations, I threw a wad of money on the counter and bolted out into the heat. To make the train, I would have to sprint the whole way, but I couldn't sprint for long, not after the lunch I had just eaten. Indeed, just breathing was uncomfortable. Even so, I struggled along, probably looking like some God-forsaken refugee with my distended belly and Quasimodo gait. At the Superdome, I steeled myself and ran the rest of the way to Union Terminal and arrived just in time to hear, "Last call for the *Sunset Limited*!" There were two long lines of people, tickets in hand, waiting to be checked into the boarding area, but I ran seemingly unnoticed right past them and the ticket punchers, proving, perhaps, that joggers have finally joined the ranks of winos and stray dogs as invisible creatures of the street.

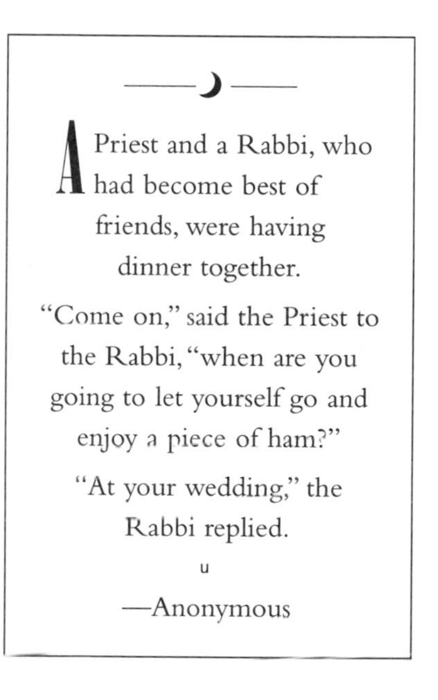

A Priest and a Rabbi, who had become best of friends, were having dinner together.

"Come on," said the Priest to the Rabbi, "when are you going to let yourself go and enjoy a piece of ham?"

"At your wedding," the Rabbi replied.

—Anonymous

As I closed my cabin door, the train began to jolt, then gather speed and, moments later, Mr. Graham knocked, then asked, "You want me to bring lunch to your cabin?"

I said, "Dear God, no." Even the slightest movement on my part, I feared, would introduce Mr. Graham to the lunch I had just eaten.

"You been out running, that's good. Skip a meal and exercise. Being healthy, that's my man!"

Later, when I could move, I told Mr. Graham about almost being late for the train. He was not surprised. "New Orleans, that's a train-missing town. Happens most every trip."

This trip, too, I learned. Three people missed the train, and they will have to fly to San Antonio to re-board.

The Dining Car seats seventy-two at a serving, four to a table, so each meal I eat with three new people—which means that I am already on a friendly, first name basis with nearly two dozen fellow passengers. Now, when I pass one of them in the observation car, or meet one downstairs at the snack bar, they unfailingly ask one of two questions. The most common question is, "You think we'll ever get out of Texas?" which is their way of joking about the monotony of the landscape.

For myself, I like Texas. I like the space and the light, and the way cloud shadows gather speed, sailing across the yellow plains. I like the look of the one-windmill ranch houses and the way, in this dry country, the passage of a pickup truck can be marked by its contrail of dust. It is a land so desolate that the isolated strongholds of human existence assume worth and a heightened interest. From each infrequent house, children come running out to wave at our train and, an hour ago, in the middle of nowhere, a woman paused beneath a clothesline to catch my eye and smile—or so I choose to believe, for she was very pretty in her flowered dress. Her face was lean and wind blushed, and the unaffected way she tossed her straw hair back communicated an attitude of weathered acceptance. She lived in a mobile home with a fence and a clothesline, and she could still smile at a train. To me, she is one of the many things attractive about Texas, and a reason that I do not answer the question, "You think we'll ever get out of Texas?"

A question I do answer (though I'm always taken aback when it is asked) is, "How's your frog doing?" I have been asked that nine or ten times in the course of the day; clearly, word has gotten out, and I have only myself to blame. When I started the trip, I thought it would be fun to ask people I met along the way to help me name the frog—not that I believe amphibians should be named, I don't. It has been my experience that frogs revel in anonymity, and I had no desire to degrade my jumping frog or his species. Still, asking new friends to suggest a name seemed a way to allow them to share my journey, so that's what I did. Anne and Mark thought Chief Osceola was a good name. "After the famous Florida Indian chief," Anne explained. William, an Australian I met in the dining car, thought I should call the frog Roo. "Roo as in kangaroo," he said. "You ever seen those bastards jump?" A woman who boarded in New Orleans said I should name the frog Huey P. Long. "Long jump—get it?" I complimented each suggestion warmly, for the names said more about the namer than the frog, which is what I had hoped in the first place. Still, I have yet to use a name when addressing the frog for the simple reason that I have had no cause, or desire, to speak with it.

Tonight I had cause to speak with the frog.

Twice a day, I open the Tupperware box to change the frog's towel, soaking it first with spring water so that the frog will stay cool and damp. Then I toss in a few crickets—always wordlessly, for the frog's stoicism does not inspire conversation. He sits motionless, his throat pouch pulsing steady as a heartbeat, and he still does not move when I reseal the lid. Which is why, tonight, I decided to see if I could make him jump. I was taking him to a famous jumping frog contest, after all, but since acquiring him from a Florida swamp, I had yet to see the damn thing move. So I placed the towel on the floor, placed the frog on the towel, then sat back to gauge his athletic ability.

Nothing. The frog sat there yellow eyed and indifferent.

I touched his back legs, and still he did not move.

For the first time, I spoke to the frog: "Three thousand miles on a train just so you can embarrass me and the whole state of Florida! Come on, jump!"

I turned to get the bottle of water—maybe he needed dampening—but when I turned back, the frog was gone. That quick, he had disappeared. I looked under the bed, under the chair, looked in the shower, even looked in the Tupperware box. No frog. When I saw that I had left my cabin door open, I got down on my hands and knees and crawled out into the hall which is when I realized with a dawning sense of dread that there was a two-inch crack beneath the door of every sleeper—my frog could easily slip into any room on the train.

I didn't panic. After another careful search of my own quarters, I went to get help. With minutes, William from Australia was crawling around the west end of the coach, and Celeste, of Louisiana, was duck walking the east end, shining a little flashlight. The situation was compromising enough, but then I heard William call, "Roo? Where are ya', Roo!" and, from the other end, I heard Celeste urging, "Oh, Huey-y-y. Come here, Huey-y-y."

I got their attention and held my finger to my lips. William nodded as if he understood, but he didn't understand because, in a softer voice, he began to call, "Roo-o-o? Show yerself, ya' bloody little reptile!"

Terrible. I pictured Mr. Graham arriving unexpectedly and demanding an explanation. I pictured us being put off the train—and New Mexico is no place for a frog. I called off the search. I got a can of beer and closed my cabin door—it would dull the screams I would inevitably hear when some neighbor awakened to find a full-grown bullfrog sitting on her chest. A half hour passed, maybe an hour. I sat looking out at the stratified darkness of the American west. Then I heard, hu-RHUMP.

The frog was at my feet. I reached to grab him, but he loped away in a series of very fast jumps, but no distance to them at all. When I finally caught him, I said, "You bastard, a snake could outjump you!"

As always, the frog was stoic to the point of indifference—which, in truth, made him an otherwise ideal companion for train travel.

It was somewhere near New Orleans that a nice lady named Winifred who, upon hearing that I planned to spend a day exploring Arizona, first mentioned Sedona. She said it was a strange and splendid town; the place she had been united with the many quartz shards she wore on her wrists and around her neck. "Crystals," she called them, and took the time to explain their significance. "They help focus my aura," she told me. "They are my conduit to the cosmic source. It has to do with our physical bodies being tuned to the electromagnetic field of the earth. You know about that, of course?"

I didn't, but, as a professional explorer and outdoorsman, I felt obligated to listen.

"Like human radios," Winifred explained. "The earth constantly transmits an electromagnetic signal—that's why many people feel more at home outdoors than indoors. And because these crystals are from Sedona, they produce much stronger vibrations because Sedona is a power spot; a focal point for the earth's electromagnetic energies. Not a different frequency, just stronger."

The same voltage, but a stronger amperage, I suggested—as a farm boy, I had been zapped many times by cattle prods and electric fencing, so was intimately familiar with the distinction.

Winifred was delighted with my analogy; said she had never heard the complexities of Sedona grasped so quickly. "That kind of quick insight isn't commonplace," she said. "You really must visit Sedona—I think my crystals are already having an effect on you."

Unlikely but, just to be safe, I avoided Winifred for the rest of the trip. But then I met Mr. Danby, a gray-haired gentleman in a baggy brown suit who, one night in the observation car, eased down beside me, straightened his rope tie, and asked, "You made any sightings, yet?"—an odd question, normally, but we were just west of Alpine, Texas, entering an expanse of desert where, for many decades, lights of an unknown source have been seen but never explained—the Marfa Ghost Lights, they are called.

I had been looking for the lights, true, but instead of answering the man, I only shrugged my shoulders and said, "Sightings?"

That was all the encouragement Mr. Danby needed. "Unidentified Flying Objects," he replied. "The Amtrak tour pamphlet has it all wrong. People have been seeing strange lights in this desert for a hundred years, but they aren't ghosts, they're UFOs—it's those blasted extraterrestrials! They terrorize west Texas, but the government won't do a thing about it. Afraid the citizenry will panic! And if you think it's bad here, you ought to spend a few days in Sedona, Arizona. Heck, the UFOs spotted here are probably lost and just looking for Sedona, because that's where they have to go to recharge their ships with telluric energy. There are two or three sightings on a slow night in Sedona, and don't even ask about the number of abductions."

So I didn't ask. But, later in the conversation, I did mention that I planned to spend a day or two roaming around Arizona—a thing which made Mr. Danby oddly suspicious. "You ever been to Arizona before?" he asked.

"No."

"You have any reason to leave the train there? Business, maybe? Allergies? Got relatives in the Biosphere?"

"No."

Mr. Danby leaned forward and seemed to study me closely. "You ever suffered unaccountable lapses in memory? Ever dreamed of being locked in a capsule with a strange-looking creature?"

Evidently, he could read the truth in my expression, so I tried to hastily explain, "It's because I've been traveling with a frog; he's in my sleeper right now—"

"Gad almighty!" Mr. Danby exclaimed. "I knew it the moment I laid eyes on you!"

What it was he knew, Mr. Danby wouldn't come right out and say, but it was easy enough to piece together the implications: I wasn't getting off in Arizona voluntarily—the extraterrestrials were directing my movements. I was being called for reinspection, much like a faulty automobile. At least, that's the way I read it.

"Take my advice, son," Mr. Danby said. "Whatever you do, no matter how hard you got to fight it, do not go to Sedona!"

What rational, reasonable human being could ignore such a warning?

In less than twenty-four hours, driving a white rental car, my frog on the front seat beside me, I was crossing that peculiar town's city limits.

Sedona lies on a branch of the Verde River, a stunning region of earth tones and arroyo greens, all backdropped by red rock spires; the stalagmite remnants of geologic cataclysm that, when isolated by morning sunlight, or smudged by darkness, form a Stonehenge perimeter around a town that some recognize as the hub of New Age Geomancy and Holistic Crystal Spiritualism—a thing that means much to a few, but meant nothing at all to me or the frog on the afternoon of our arrival.

To me, Sedona looked like any other affluent Arizona outpost town. Houses, with their red tile roofs, were new and of a type: block and stucco or river rock, with lawns displaying a desert tableau of stone and cactus, as neat as Japanese gardens. Aside from being uncommonly pretty, there seemed to be nothing peculiar about it—an observation a gas station attendant I met was quick to confirm: "People come here thinking this is a town of weirdos. It's not. Mostly, it's a friendly, hard-working kind of place."

What is different about Sedona, though, is that a thriving tourist industry has developed around the belief that the town lies on or near ten major "vortices," which are said to be geological anomalies that are the focal points of the earth's electromagnetic energies. The gas station attendant didn't tell me this—I read it in a book at the New Age Center, which was just down the street from a long line of New Age bookstores, retail crystal fitters, pyramid palaces, and a pink Jeep tour company that offered: Healing Ceremonies, Sacred Places Pilgrimages, and maps to Vortex Power Spots.

Even if I wasn't being summoned by extraterrestrials, a town like this was too good to pass up.

I spent what I thought was to be my only full day in Sedona visiting some of the places recommended to me by the New Age Center. I had a "life reading" at the Spiritualist's Fair where I was told that I had been a medieval monk in a previous life, and that I now had seven guardian spirits looking after me, almost twice the normal number—happy news, considering my lifestyle. I attended a Hopi festival. I listened to Swiss vocalists singing special healing notes, akin (if I heard right) to the microtonal music of extraterrestrials. After all of this, I spent half an hour sitting beneath a copper pyramid where, if nothing else, I was impressed by the way it sharpened my thirst.

After a pleasant search for beverages, I stopped at a few of the New Age bookstores where, I must admit, I finally did notice something unusual about Sedona: almost every person I met was part Indian. It's true. Not that I could discern their genealogy with my eyes, no. I didn't have to because they came right out and told me, and usually very early on in the conversation. I met part Lakotas, part Apaches, part Hopis, nearly all of whom had Nordic features despite their antecedents, except for one who looked Italian. Yet their heritage was readily visible in the sweeping hand gestures they used to describe the powers of the vortices, their quest as spiritual warriors, and also to give directions. It's a kind of Indian sign language—I know from having watched many Westerns on television.

"All people in this country are searching for something," one of the bookstore Indians told me.

Who was I to disagree?

My day in Sedona was interesting and enjoyable, but enough was enough, plus I was on a timetable. So I returned to my room at the New Earth Lodge, loaded my backpack and frog into the car, and headed out. But at a gas station at the edge of town something happened that my life reader had not predicted, and the pyramid had not premonished: I encountered Mr. Danby a second time.

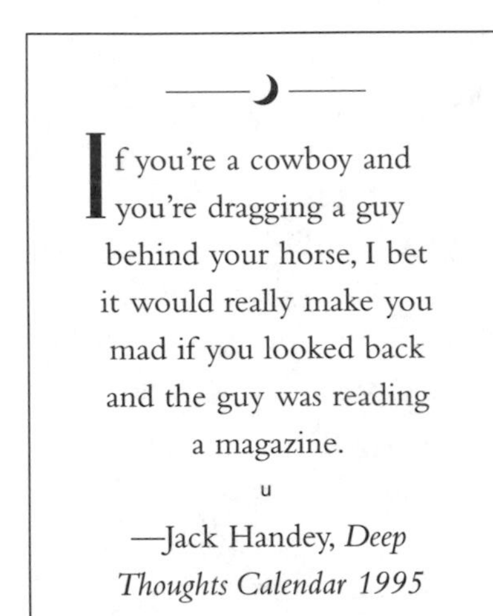

If you're a cowboy and you're dragging a guy behind your horse, I bet it would really make you mad if you looked back and the guy was reading a magazine.

—Jack Handey, *Deep Thoughts Calendar 1995*

Danby had been planning to come to Sedona all along—that's why he was on the train. "UFOs have been my hobby for twenty years," he said to me. "I first learned of all the ET activity in Sedona from the Armstrong newsletter, and I've been coming here ever since."

Meaning the *Armstrong Report*, published by Sedona's Virgil Armstrong, whose book, *ETs and UFOs: They Need Us, We Don't Need Them*, is said, by some, to be the definitive account of Sedona's special relationship with visitors from outer space. (I would later talk with Armstrong—an articulate man, who asked me to pass along this warning: "The frenetic energy created by a nation of untethered people invites alien visitors. They could take over at any time!")

Yet, I hadn't seen a single ET or a UFO, which is what I told Mr. Danby.

"Then come along with me tomorrow night, and I'll guarantee you'll see one, maybe both—if you're willing to run the risk."

Personal risk, of course, means nothing to me, but staying an extra day would mean that I would have to miss the Calaveras Jumping Frog Contest which, to be honest, was an increasingly attractive proposition. Here's why: my frog couldn't jump. Oh, he could hop around fast enough if I was chasing him, but he lacked the athlete's gift of explosive power. He didn't have, I had gradually admitted to myself, that championship fiber described by some as "The look of eagles." Matched against those California frogs, he would humiliate both of us and, worse, embarrass our home state of Florida.

Mr. Danby sweetened the offer by adding, "Bring the frog with you. One night on a vortex will change you both. You'll see a UFO, and your frog will be able to jump ten, maybe twenty feet. The ionic energy boost in those places is amazing!"

The next night, carrying the frog in his box, I met Mr. Danby at what locals call the Airport Vortex (because it's right next to the Sedona Airport) where we followed him up a path, then climbed onto a high saddle of sandstone that overlooked the Verde Valley. I should say right here that those of us who have not evolved spiritually—or who didn't have the foresight to buy a map—would never be able to find a vortex on our own because they look like any other place, just rock and dirt and a few wind-battered bushes.

"It's what's going on beneath us that makes this place a vortex," Mr. Danby said as we sat down to wait. "Underneath these rocks are veins of iron and basalt running through old lava flows. They release electrical energy—the 'corona discharge effect,' it's called—which energizes our physical and psychic abilities, and also attracts ETs because they need the power to recharge their ships. We must sit very quietly and reverently for a few minutes and you'll be able to feel the ions entering your body."

I sat quietly for a time but felt nothing, so I burped open the lid of the frog's box so the ions could get to him. Having grown up in swamps, maybe he was more attuned to the earth's energy than I. That quick, the frog hopped past my fingers and escaped. He jumped away in the darkness while I scrambled in pursuit, slapping my hands on the rocks behind him always a microsecond too late.

I heard Mr. Danby say softly, "I'll be go to hell. He really does have a frog."

Not at that moment I didn't. The animal wasn't strong, true, but he was quick, and he led me on a zigzag chase across the sandstone...and then suddenly disappeared. I stood staring dumbly after him until I realized what had happened.

I turned to Danby and yelled, "My frog just jumped off the damn cliff!"

It was true. I went to the edge and looked over the precipice where, twenty feet below, all was dark and still.

I wasn't in the mood for silence or reverence now. I was angry. That frog and I had covered a lot of miles together, and I liked him about as much as a person can like a frog—which, granted, isn't all that much. Still, he was a good frog, and he had no pretenses. He was what he was—a thing that is rare, particularly in people during these frenetic times. But now Danby's absurd promises had made a fool of me and gotten my frog smushed.

I grabbed a flashlight and hustled back down the path, then circled around the spire to the area where the frog should have landed. Above me, I could hear Danby yelling something—what, I didn't understand or care—and then he began to shine his light around the base of the precipice. After only maybe five minutes, I located the frog.

He was alive. He sat there blinking in the glare of light. When I reached to catch him, he made a dozen or so spirited hops. The fall hadn't hurt him a bit and, as if to demonstrate, he bolted toward what appeared to be another cliff.

To the frog, I said, "You dumb ass," and then I carried him back up the path where Mr. Danby, not at all excited, told me a UFO had arrived at the moment of my departure.

"You didn't see their searchlight?" he asked. "Apparently, the ETs like you. They were trying to help."

"Uh-huh," I said. All I wanted to do was get the frog's box, my car, and get back on the road.

"Did you ever think you'd see that frog jump twenty-feet—and live?" Danby pressed. "I'm telling you, it's the power of the vortex! The vortex healed that animal, then attracted the extraterrestrials to help you find him."

As I was leaving, Danby told me that things like that happened all the time. "It's what makes the place special," he said.

*Randy Wayne White is the author of several novels and works of nonfiction and is a contributing editor for* Outside *magazine. He's covered the America's Cup races in Australia, and has written about Sumatra, Singapore, Central America, Vietnam, Borneo, Malaysia, Ireland, the Cayman and Windward Islands, and South America. He has dog-sledded in Alaska and brought back refugees from Cuba. He lives in Florida.*

TODD McEWEN

# They Tell Me You Are Big

*When the plane landed, he had gone over to the Far Side.*

THE TECHNOLOGICAL PARADE OF WELCOME: I WAS ALREADY dead with fatigue. Thank you for flying with us today, here is your ticket, change planes in Chicago, you'll have to change planes in Chicago, change in Chicago. They said it so often I began to get the idea I should change planes in Chicago. *Change planes*: the phrase began to lose any reference to travel; it acquired a dread phenomenological taint. But I did not change those sorts of planes in Chicago. Rather, in Chicago I *changed size*. For when I deplaned (more tech-talk) I walked into Big People Land.

I was obliged to go a short distance through a glass tube, the story of a life, from one gate to another. I then had an hour, a whole, giant hour to myself. In Big People Land. And there they were. They were all about me: large surely moving salesmen and mammoth middle managers, corn-fed beef-fed farm-bred monuments to metabolism. Flying from dairy states to beef capitals to commodities centers. From Fon du Lac to Dubuque, their huge briefcases *stuffed with meat*.

Clinching beefy deals with muscular handshakes. Their faces were florid Mt. Rushmores with aviator spectacles and sideburns uniformly metallic; their eyes, bovine, the size of Dutch plates, reflected their Low Country ancestries. Their hands were steam shovels, their shoes big as our tiny neurotic New York family car. I'm not talking fat, although flesh is essential in Chicago. I'm talking big-boned, as the apologists say. I, a tiny undernourished New York worrier, had been injected into the enlarged heart of America.

Airports like abattoirs are white. All this moving meat, these great bodies laughing, phoning, making valuable contacts, astonished me. I was overwhelmed by the size of everything and everybody, their *huge bigness*! I had to sit down. But where? Everything I sat in dwarfed, *engulfed* me. I was a baby opossum, writhing in a tablespoon in a Golden Nature Guide. I felt fear, tininess, and hunger. I decided the only way to become as big as the Big People was to begin eating.

In the infinite coffee shop, my eyes struggled to take in the polyptych menu and its thousand offerings. Eggs with legs, friendly forks and spoons marched across it. GOOD MORNING! *Barnyard Suggestions*... What! I thought. Wanna meet this chicken in the hayloft in half an hour, fella? But these were not that kind of barnyard suggestion. Here in Big People Land, land-o-lotsa wholesomeness, they were suggesting I eat the following: **(1)** 3 strips of bacon, 2 pancakes, 2 eggs (any style), 2 sausages, juice, toast, and coffee; **(2)** 6 strips of bacon, 5 pancakes, 4 eggs (any style), 3 sausages, juice, toast, and coffee; or **(3)** 12 strips of bacon, 9 pancakes, 7 eggs (any style), 1½ gallons of juice, 3 lbs. of toast, and a "Bottomless Pit" (which I took to be a typographical error for "Pot") of coffee. Thus emptying any barnyard I could imagine of all life. Again I was lost. I felt I was visiting Karnak. I pleaded for half an order of toast, eight pieces.

Outside the window, far away, Chicago was dawning. Obsidian towers, an Art Deco pipe organ sprouting from the gold prairie, Lake Michigan still dark beyond. A brachycephalic woman was seated opposite me, biting big things. Her teeth were the size of horse teeth. She said we could see into the next state. She was eating such big things and so quickly, a wind was blowing at our table. I turned from this and peered out through the clear air, into the next state. In the far distance I saw great shapes which I knew weren't mountains but my giant Midwestern relatives I am too small ever to visit.

Now I was filled with huge toast. I crawled, miniscule, back through the tubes to the gate. I bought a newspaper and my money looked puny and foreign in the vendor's big paw. In the chairs of Big People Land, my feet never touched the floor. I began to open the *Sun-Times*. But. It was big. Here it wasn't even Sunday and I was suddenly engaged in a desperate battle with what seemed to be a colossal duvet, a *mural* made of incredibly stiff paper. It unfolded and unfolded. It was a whale passing by, it covered me and all my possessions. It surged over the pillar ashtray and began to creep like fog over the gentleman next to me. Help, I said. 'Scuse me, watch your paper there, he said. *His tongue was the size of my dog.*

I was exhausted. I could do nothing but wait for my plane to be announced. I watched the Big People. What is it like to move about the world, to travel, free of the fears of the tiny: the fear of being crushed by all the big things Big People make and use? Not just newspapers and barnyard suggestions and airplanes but their Big Companies and their Eternal Truths and the endless statistics of baseball.

The airport was hugely hot with Big People warmth. Warmth from the roaring heaters of their big roaring cars, from the blazing campfires of their substantial vacations. And I thought perhaps a few of these Big People were glowing not only from tremendous breakfasts and the excitement and reward of business but from their still-warm still-tousled beds of large love.

*Todd McEwen is the author of three novels,* Fisher's Hornpipe, Who Sleeps with Katz, *and* McX: A Romance of the Dour, *which won a Scottish Arts Council award in 1991. He lives in Edinburgh with his wife, novelist Lucy Ellman.*

The first to intrude on my dream world was a dowdy creature, who sat nursing an engineering textbook on a seat a short distance away. I could see him eyeing me up for a while before he actually put down *Elementary Engineering Drawing*, and came over to me.

"*Crime and Punishment*," he said. "What is this?"

"It is a novel," I said.

"You are studying this book?"

"No, I'm reading it for pleasure."

"Why pleasure?"

It was a good question. It wasn't one of those novels that particularly improved on third reading.

"Well, I suppose I rather enjoy reading novels."

He eyed me suspiciously.

"What," he asked, "is your qualification?"

—William Dalrymple, *In Xanadu*

DOUGLAS ADAMS AND
MARK CARWARDINE

# The Transit Lounge Shuffle

*Stopping in Tanzania, these travelers just can't get it right.*

THE AIRCRAFT TRUNDLED TO A HALT OUTSIDE A SORT OF BUS shelter which served Mwanza as an airport, and we were told we had to disembark for half an hour and go and wait in the "international transit lounge."

This consisted of a large concrete shed with two fair-sized rooms in it connected by a corridor. The building had a kind of bombed appearance to it—some of the walls were badly crushed and had tangles of rusty iron spilling from their innards and through the elderly travel posters of Italy pasted over them. We moved in for half an hour, hefted our bags of camera equipment to the floor, and slumped over the battered plastic seats. I dug out a cigarette, and Mark dug out his Nikon F3 and MD4 motor drive to photograph me smoking it. There was little else to do.

After a moment or two a man in brown polyester looked in at us, did not at all like the look of us, and asked us if we were transit passengers. We said we were. He shook his head with infinite weariness and told us that if we were transit passengers, then we were supposed to be in the other of the two rooms. We were obviously very crazy and stupid not to have realized this. He stayed there lumped against the doorjamb, raising his eyebrows pointedly at us until we eventually gathered our gear together and dragged it off down the corridor to the other room. He watched us go past him, shaking his head in wonder and sorrow at the stupid futility of the human condition in general and ours in particular, and then closed the door behind us.

The second room was identical to the first. Identical in all respects other than one, which was that it had a hatchway let into one wall. A large, vacant-looking girl was leaning through it with her elbows on the counter and her fists jammed up into her cheekbones. She was watching some flies crawling up the wall, not with any great interest because they were not doing anything unexpected, but at least they were doing something. Behind her was a table stacked with biscuits, chocolate bars, cola, and a pot of coffee, and we headed straight toward this like a pack of stoats. Just before we reached it, however, we were suddenly headed off by a man in blue polyester, who asked us what we thought we were doing in there. We explained that we were transit passengers on our way to Zaire, and he looked at us as if we had completely taken leave of our senses.

"*Transit* passengers?" he said. "It is not allowed for transit passengers to be in here." He waved us magnificently away from the snack counter, made us pick up all our gear again, and herded us back through the door and away into the first room, where a minute later the man in the brown polyester found us again.

He looked at us.

Slow incomprehension engulfed him, followed by sadness,

anger, deep frustration, and a sense that the world had been created specifically to cause him vexation. He leaned back against the wall, frowned, closed his eyes, and pinched the bridge of his nose.

"You are in the wrong room," he said simply. "You are transit passengers. Please go to the other room."

There is a wonderful calm that comes over you in such situations, particularly when there is a refreshment kiosk involved. We nodded, picked up our gear in a Zen-like manner, and made our way back down the corridor to the other room. Here the man in blue polyester accosted us once more, but we patiently explained to him that he could fuck off. We needed chocolate, we needed coffee, maybe even a reviving packet of biscuits, and what was more, we intended to have them. We outfaced him, dumped our bags on the ground, walked firmly up to the counter, and hit a major unforeseen snag.

The girl wouldn't sell us anything. She seemed surprised that we even bothered to raise the subject. With her fists still jammed into her cheekbones, she shook her head slowly at us and continued to watch the flies on the wall.

The problem, it gradually transpired after a conversation which flowed like gum from a tree, was this. She would only accept Tanzanian currency. She knew without needing to ask that we didn't have any, for the simple reason that no one ever did. This was an international transit lounge, and the airport had no currency-exchange facilities, therefore no one who came in here could possibly have any Tanzanian currency and therefore she couldn't serve them.

After a few minutes of futile wrangling, we had to accept the flawless simplicity of her argument and just sit out our time there gloomily eyeing the coffee and chocolate bars, while our pockets bulged with useless dollars, sterling, French francs, and Kenyan shillings. The girl stared vacantly at the flies, obviously resigned to the fact that she never did any business at all. After a while we became quite interested in watching the flies as well

At last, we were told that our flight was ready to depart again, and we returned to our planeload of missionaries.

*Douglas Adams was the author of* Hitchhiker's Guide to the Galaxy, *a novel which originated from his radio series of the same name. In 1980,* Hitchhiker's Guide to the Galaxy *was placed on the American Library Association's Best Books for Young Adults List. He also wrote with Mark Carwardine,* Last Chance to See, *from which this story was excerpted. Adams died in 2001 after suffering a heart attack at a gym in Santa Monica, California.*

*

"Ah, yes, view is very best from there. You can see all three pyramids in a line, you can see the Sphinx, the Nile, and all of Cairo. But no walk," he said. "Is too far. You need camel." He turned to look admiringly at his beast. It is said that the Koran contains ninety-nine names for Allah, and that the camel looks so smug because he alone knows the one hundredth.

"Do you read Arabic?" I asked the man. Some of his colleagues had not.

"Yes, of course."

I showed him the note I had, on a sudden inspiration, asked my hotel manager to write in Arabic at the back of my notebook earlier that morning: I HAVE VERY BAD HEMORRHOIDS. I CAN NOT POSSIBLY SIT ON A CAMEL.

—Brad Newsham, *Take Me With You: A Round-the-World Journey to Invite a Stranger Home*

DONALD KATZ

* * *

# The King of the Ferret-Leggers

*It takes an iron will to keep 'em down.*

MR. REG MELLOR, THE "KING OF FERRET-LEGGING," PACED across his tiny Yorkshire miner's cottage as he explained the rules of the English sport that he has come to dominate rather late in life. "Ay lad," said the seventy-two-year-old champion, "no jockstraps allowed. No underpants—nothin' whatever. And it's no good with tight trousers, mind ye. Little bah-stards have to be able to move around inside there from ankle to ankle."

Some eleven years ago I first heard of the strange pastime called ferret-legging, and for a decade since then I have sought a publication possessed of sufficient intelligence and vision to allow me to travel to northern England in search of the fabled players of the game.

Basically the contest involves the tying of a competitor's trousers at the ankles and the subsequent insertion into those trousers of a couple of peculiarly vicious fur-coated, foot-long carnivores called ferrets. The brave contestant's belt is then pulled tight, and he proceeds to stand there in front of the judges as long as he can, while animals with claws like hypodermic needles and teeth like number sixteen carpet tacks try their damndest to get out.

From a dark and obscure past, the sport has made an astonishing comeback in the past fifteen years. When I first heard about ferret-legging, the world record stood at forty painful seconds of "keepin' 'em down," as they say in ferret-legging circles. A few years later the dreaded one-minute mark was finally surpassed. The current record—implausible as it may seem—now stands at an awesome five hours and twenty-six minutes, a mark reached last year by the gaudily tattooed seventy-two-year-old little Yorkshireman with the waxed military mustache who now stood two feet away from me in the middle of the room, apparently undoing his trousers.

"The ferrets must have a full mouth o' teeth," Reg Mellor said as he fiddled with his belt. "No filing of the teeth; no clipping. No dope for you or the ferrets. You must be sober, and the ferrets must be hungry—though any ferret'll eat yer eyes out even if he isn't hungry."

Reg Mellor lives several hours north of London atop the thick central seam of British coal that once fueled the most powerful surge into modernity in the world's history. He lives in the city of Barnsley, home to a quarter-million downtrodden souls, and the brunt of many derisive jokes in Great Britain. Barnsley was the subject of much national mirth recently when "the most grievously mocked town in Yorkshire"—a place people drive miles out of their way to circumvent—opened a tourist information center. Everyone thought that was a good one.

When I stopped at the tourist office and asked the astonished woman for a map, she said, "Ooooh, a mup ees it, luv? No mups 'ere. Noooo." She did, however, know the way to

Reg Mellor's house. Reg is, after all, Barnsley's only reigning king.

Finally, then, after eleven long years, I sat in front of a real ferret-legger, a man among men. He stood now next to a glowing fire of Yorkshire coal as I tried to interpret the primitive record of his long life, which is etched in tattoos up and down his thick arms. Reg finally finished explaining the technicalities of this burgeoning sport.

"So then, lad. Any more questions for I poot a few down for ye?"

"Yes, Reg."

"Ay, whoot then?"

"Well, Reg," I said. "I think people in America will want to know. Well...since you don't wear any protection...and, well, I've heard a ferret can bite your thumb off. Do they ever—you know?"

Reg's stiff mustache arched toward the ceiling under a sly grin. "You really want to know what they get up to down there, eh?" Reg said, looking for all the world like some working man's Long John Silver. "Well, take a good look."

Then Reg Mellor let his trousers fall around his ankles.

A short digression: A word is in order concerning ferrets, a weasel-like animal well known to Europeans but, because of the near extinction of the black-footed variety in the American West, not widely known in the United States.

Alternatively referred to by professional ferret handlers as "shark-of-the-land," a "piranha with feet," "fur-coated evil," and "the only four-legged creature in existence that kills just for kicks," the common domesticated ferret—*Mustela putorius*—has the spinal flexibility of a snake and the jaw musculature of a pit bull. Rabbits, rats, and even frogs run screaming from hiding places when confronted with a ferret. Ferreters—those who hunt with ferrets, as opposed to putting them in their pants—sit around and tell tales of rabbits running toward hunters to surrender after gazing into the torch-red eyes of an oncoming ferret.

Before they were outlawed in New York State in the early part of the century, ferrets were used to exterminate rats. A ferret with a string on its leg, it was said, could knock off more than a hundred street-wise New York City rats twice its size in an evening.

> You know you're getting old when you stoop to tie your shoes and wonder what else you can do while you're down there.
>
> —George Burns

In England, the amazing rise of ferret-legging pales before the new popularity of keeping ferrets as pets, a trend replete with numerous tragic consequences. A baby was killed and eaten in 1978, and several children have been mauled by ferrets every year since then.

Loyal to nothing that lives, the ferret has only one characteristic that might be deemed positive—a tenacious, single-minded belief in finishing whatever it starts. That usually entails biting *off* whatever it bites. The rules of ferret-legging allow the leggers to try to knock the ferret off a spot it's biting (from outside the trouser only), but that is no small matter, as ferrets never let go. No less a source than the *Encyclopædia Britannica* suggests that you can get a ferret to let go by pressing a certain spot over its eye, but Reg Mellor and the other ferret specialists I talked to all say that is absurd.

Reg favors a large screwdriver to get a ferret off his finger. Another ferret-legger told me that a ferret that had almost dislodged his left thumb let go only after the ferret and the man's thumb were held under scalding tap water—for ten minutes.

Mr. Graham Wellstead, the head of the British Ferret and Ferreting Society, says that little is known of the diseases carried by the ferret because veterinarians are afraid to touch them.

Reg Mellor, a man who has been more intimate with ferrets than many men have been with their wives, calls ferrets "cannibals, things that live only to kill, that'll eat your eyes out to get at your brain" at their worst, and "untrustworthy" at their very best.

Reg says he observed with wonder the growing popularity of ferret-legging throughout the seventies. He had been hunting with ferrets in the verdant moors and dales outside of Barnsley for much of a century. Since a cold and wet ferret exterminates with a little less enthusiasm than a dry one, Reg used to keep his ferrets in his pants for hours when he hunted in the rain—and it always rained where he hunted.

"The world record was sixty seconds. Sixty seconds! I can stick a ferret up me ass longer than that."

So at sixty-nine, Reg Mellor found his game. As he stood in front of me now, naked from the waist down, Reg looked every bit a champion.

"So look close," he said again.

I did look, at an incredible tattoo of a zaftig woman on Reg's thigh. His legs appeared crosshatched with scars. But I refused to "look close," saying something about not being paid enough for that.

"Come on, Reg," I said. "Do they bite your—you know?"

"Do they?" he thundered with irritation as he pulled up his pants. "Why, I had 'em hangin' off me—"

Reg stopped short because a woman who was with me, a London television reporter, had entered the cottage. I suddenly feared that I would never know from what the raging ferrets dangle. Reg offered my friend a chair with the considerable gallantry of a man who had served in the Queen's army for more than twenty years. Then he said to her, "Are you cheeky, luv?"

My friend looked confused.

"Say yes," I hissed.

"Yes."

"Why," Reg roared again, "I had 'em hangin' from me tool for hours an' hours an' hours! Two at a time—one on each side. I been swelled up big as that!" Reg pointed to a five-pound can of instant coffee.

I then made the mistake of asking Reg Mellor if his age allowed him the impunity to be the most daring ferret-legger in the world.

"And what do ye mean by that?" he said.

"Well, I just thought since you probably aren't going to have any more children...."

"Are you sayin' I ain't pokin' 'em for sure?"

A small red hut sits in an overgrown yard outside Reg Mellor's door. "Come outa there, ye bah-stards," Reg yelled as he flailed around the inside of the hut looking for some ferrets that had just arrived a few hours earlier. He emerged with two dirty white animals, which he held quite firmly by their necks. They both had fearsome unblinking eyes as hard and red as rubies.

Reg thrust one of them at me, and I suddenly thought that he intended the ferret to avenge my faux pas concerning his virility: so I began to run for a fence behind which my television friend was already standing because she refused to watch. Reg finally got me to take one of the ferrets by its steel cable of a neck while he tied his pants at the ankle and prepared to "put 'em down."

A young man named Malcolm, with a punk haircut, came into the yard on a motorbike. "You puttin' 'em down again, Reg?" Malcolm asked.

Reg took the ferret from my bloodless hand and stuck the beast's head deep into his mouth.

"Oh yuk, Reg," said Malcolm.

Reg pulled the now-quite-embittered-looking ferret out of his mouth and stuffed it and another ferret into his pants. He cinched his belt tight, clenched his fists at his sides, and gazed up into the gray Yorkshire firmament in what I guessed could only be a gesture of prayer. Claws and teeth now protruded all over Reg's hyperactive trousers. The two bulges circled round and round one leg, getting higher and higher, and finally...they went up and over to the other leg.

"Thank God," I said.

"Yuk, Reg," said Malcolm.

"The claws," I managed, "Aren't they sharp, Reg?"

"Ay," said Reg laconically. "Ay."

Reg Mellor gives all the money he makes from ferret-legging to the local children's home. As with all great champions, he has also tried to bring more visibility to the sport that has made him famous. One Mellor innovation is the introduction of white trousers at major competitions ("shows the blood better").

Mellor is a proud man. Last year he retired from professional ferret-legging in disgust after attempting to break a magic six-hour mark—the four-minute mile of ferret-legging. After five hours of having them down, Mellor found that almost all of the 2,500 spectators had gone home. Then workmen came and began to dismantle the stage, despite his protestations that he was on his way to a new record. "I'm not packing it in because I am too old or because I can't take the bites anymore." Reg told reporters after the event. "I am just too disillusioned."

One of the ferrets in Reg's pants finally poked its nose into daylight before any major damage was done, and Reg pulled the other ferret out. We all went across the road to the local pub, where everyone but Reg had a drink to calm the nerves. Reg doesn't drink. Bad for his health, he says.

Reg said he had been coaxed out of retirement recently and intends to break six—"maybe even eight"—hours within the year.

Some very big Yorkshiremen stood around us in the pub. Some of them claimed they had bitten the heads off sparrows, shrews, and even rats, but none of them would compete with Reg Mellor. One can only wonder what suffering might have been avoided if the Argentine junta had been informed that sportsmen in England put down their pants animals that are known only for their astonishingly powerful bites and their penchant for insinuating themselves into small dark holes. Perhaps the generals would have reconsidered their actions on the Falklands.

But Reg Mellor refuses to acknowledge that his talent is made of the stuff of heroes, of a mixture of indomitable pride, courage, concentration, and artless grace. "Naw noon o' that," said the king. "You just got be able ta have your tool bitten and not care."

*

*Donald Katz is an author, lecturer, business consultant, and founder and CEO of Audible Inc, the leading internet provider of spoken-word audio. He is the author of* Big Store: Inside the Crisis and Revolution at Sears *which won the Chicago Tribune Heartland Prize for Nonfiction. His other works include,* Home Fires: An Intimate Portrait of One Middle-Class Family in Postwar America, Just Do It: The Nike Spirit in the Corporate World, *and* The King of the Ferret Leggers and Other True Stories. *He has also served as contributing editor to* Esquire, Outside, Rolling Stone, Men's Journal, Worth, *and as a special contributor to* Sports Illustrated.

SEAN O'REILLY

* * *

# What I Did in the Doll House

*Nature was calling, with a megaphone.*

MANY YEARS AGO, I WENT TO VISIT ONE OF MY BROTHERS IN Boston. At the time he had a wonderful barn which he had converted into a two-story office and a guest house. The flooring downstairs was culled from the demolition of a local high school's gym, and the shelves were lined with books. Skylights completed the picture upstairs. It was a nice place and he was proud of it. He had not, however, due to restrictive local building codes, installed a bathroom. On the last night of my visit, I asked that the door be left open to the main house so that I might use the bathroom should any nocturnal prompting arise. I was assured that this would be done and later, I went cheerfully to bed.

I awoke early at 5:30 A.M. and although rested, felt vaguely out of focus. I attributed this to waking up in a strange place. I puttered around for fifteen or twenty minutes until nature suddenly spoke loudly that big business was at hand. I moved swiftly and quietly to the door of the main house but to my surprise, discovered that the door was locked. It was far too early to be waking everybody up, so I began to cast about for alternatives there at the crack, so to speak, of dawn. The bushes were not tall enough and there were few trees. There were also, unfortunately, many houses nearby with their lights on and the inhabitants stirring for the morning commute. Something else was also trying to commute, and it hadn't even had its coffee yet!

My anxious and barely awake consciousness was swamped with rectal messages that alternated between desperate pleading and the howling of possessed beasts. I looked about frantically, walking with clenched buttocks, and attempted to maintain composure in a rapidly disintegrating situation. The standard protocols for civilized behavior were starting to break down as they tend to in situations of extreme need. The doll house, the doll house! There was a doll house next to the barn—a bright cheerful thing of pink and yellow plastic and just large enough for an adult. I scurried inside and pleased with my newly acquired privacy released a tidal wave of fecal matter all over the floor. The stench was overpowering in the confined space of such a small area, so I made a hasty exit after performing the necessary ablutions with my t-shirt. The grotesque looseness of the still-heaving and uneven mass made me realize that it would be better if it had time to dry before I cleaned it up. I congratulated myself for finding a creative solution to my little problem and washed my hands at the hose. I thought no more about the matter and went back to the barn for an enjoyable hour of early morning reading.

Later that morning and before I left for the airport, I had a wonderful breakfast with my brother and his family. It wasn't until I got on the plane that I realized I had made no effort to clean up the mess. My fellow passengers must have thought they had a lunatic on board as I thrashed and wheezed in my seat. All I could think about on the way to Virginia was that my brother and his wife would have to tell their young children that no, they could not use the doll house because their uncle had shat in it.

*Sean O'Reilly is editor-at-large for Travelers' Tales and author of* How to Manage Your Dick: Redirect Sexual Energy and Discover Your More Spiritually Enlightened, Evolved Self.

*

My hotel in Warsaw promised a twenty-four-hour laundry service. I was impressed by the friendly backslapping of the babushkas who collect the laundry. My impression soon turned to despair when I realized that these women assumed I was donating my shirts, trousers, and other items to their collection of Western clothes. It took a few bars of Toblerone chocolate and a bottle of vodka to win my garments back.

—Peter Davis, "Room Checking"

THOM ELKJER

# The Copenhagen T-Shirt

*In this case it was more than a lowly garment.*

SOME YEARS AGO THERE WAS A JAZZ CLUB IN COPENHAGEN called Jazzhus Montmartre. One of the founders was the great saxophone player Stan Getz, and many other big-name players took their turn on the bandstand. This made it one of the few European jazz clubs that Americans knew about. So the first time I was in Copenhagen, I went to the Jazzhus Montmartre.

It was a major disappointment. By then, in the mid-'80s, the club was booking rock and roll to keep the doors open. The night I went, the band was loud and obnoxious. There weren't many people in the audience, and I didn't stay long. As I left, I noticed that the guy working the door was wearing a t-shirt with the club's name and logo.

The next morning, I got to thinking about my brother, who is not just a jazz fan, but a multitalented jazz composer, performer, and arranger. He knew about the Montmartre before I did. He was recovering from an injury back home in California. I wanted to bring him something when I came home. What could be better, I thought, than a memento from the Jazzhus Montmartre? He didn't have to know about the bad rock and roll. He would have a memento from a true temple of jazz. All I had to do was stop by the next day and pick up one of the club's t-shirts. Of course travel t-shirts are a total cliché, but this was different. This was a travel t-shirt idea with real merit.

So I went back to the club the next morning. Just before I got there I passed some kiosks selling the usual tourist stuff. I checked to see if they were selling the club's t-shirts, but they weren't, so I crossed the street and went to the front door of the club.

As at most music clubs, the door of the Jazzhus Montmartre looked like the entrance to a fortress: heavy, black, lined in metal, and sturdily locked. I knocked on the door loudly and waited a long time. Finally, I heard someone coming up the stairs, taking down a chain, unlocking locks, and sliding deadbolts. The door cracked open. It was the guy I had seen with the t-shirt the night before.

"Good morning," I said. "I'd like to buy a t-shirt."

"This is a music club," the guy said. "The t-shirts are down the street." He pointed toward the tourist kiosks. Then he closed the door and started locking the locks and bolting the bolts.

They must get some really stupid tourists in Copenhagen, because only a real idiot would bang on a heavily locked, menacingly black door with no name on it, looking for t-shirts, when there were scads of t-shirts in plain sight twenty meters away.

I knocked on the door again. The guy went through his routine with the chains and locks, and a moment later the door opened again.

"I want a Montmartre t-shirt," I said, and pointed to the one he had on.

He looked at me like I *was* a real idiot. "You want my shirt?" he asked.

"No," I said, "one like yours."

"I'm sorry, we don't sell them," he said, and closed the door.

Before he could even begin locking the locks and everything, I banged on the door again. For the third time, he opened it. Only people as well-mannered as the Danes would open the door this many times for someone they thought was stupid, or crazy, or both.

"You don't sell those shirts to people?" I asked.

"What people?" the guy asked, incredulous. "To myself?"

"No, to me. I want you to sell one to *me*."

"Sorry," he said. "They're only for the staff."

He started to close the door, but I quickly put out a hand to stop him.

"The shirt is not for me," I pleaded. "It's for my brother in America. He's a jazz musician. I was here last night, and I saw the shirts you guys wear. I know he would love to have one."

The guy opened the door a little wider. "You were here last night?" he asked. "The music was not really jazz last night. Not very good, that music."

I nodded in agreement, trying to warm this new bond between us. "So can I get a shirt for my brother?" I asked.

The guy didn't answer, but he didn't close the door. Finally he pointed to the café next door. "You can talk to the manager," he said. "He's having coffee." I thanked him, and he closed the door. I listened as he locked the locks, bolted the bolts, and refastened the chain. Then I went next door.

It was a *konditorei*, which means a small bakery café. It was brightly lit and smelled of pastry and cake. It was pretty much deserted except for three guys wearing leather jackets, sitting at a table talking. I marched up to them, asked which one was the manager of the club, and launched into my spiel. I didn't get far. As soon as I mentioned that I had been in the club the night before, he thought I wanted a refund because the band was so bad.

"I'm sorry," he said. "There was a mistake about that band. Nobody listened to their tape, so we didn't know what they played. We thought they were a different group. Did you want your money back?"

"No," I said. "I want a t-shirt."

"Or you can come to the club tonight, for free. Tonight we have a really good group, a jazz combo from France. If you want to see that group, I will let you in for free. Last night was a mistake."

"That's O.K.," I said. "I just want a t-shirt for my brother."

The manager looked at me blankly. "You want a t-shirt," he said, making sure he had heard me correctly. I nodded. He suddenly looked relieved. I wasn't an angry patron, demanding my money back. I was just a nut. He shook his head.

"Why not?" I asked.

"They're only for the staff," he said, and turned back to his companions.

People in Norway and Sweden joke that the Danes are the "Southern Europeans" of Scandinavia, which means they are more happy-go-lucky, willing to bend the rules, and so on. Apparently, though, this did not extend to jazz clubs and t-shirts. This seemed completely backwards to me. In America, jazz clubs and t-shirts rank among the more subversive elements of mainstream culture. Why were they sacrosanct in Denmark?

"The t-shirt is not for me," I said, sounding as altruistic as I could. "It's for my brother. He's a jazz musician in America, but he couldn't come here himself. I wanted to bring him a shirt from the most famous jazz club in Scandinavia!"

The manager seemed unimpressed by this little flourish, but the other two guys nodded, concurring in my judgment about the club. I plunged on. "I know the shirts are only for the staff, but this is a special case. My brother is in a tough spot right now, and it would be great if I could bring him a shirt from the club. It would really cheer him up. I won't tell anyone in Denmark about buying the shirt. I promise."

I once flew from Melbourne to Belgrade with Yugoslav Airlines. The large woman who sat next to me had never flown before, but she seemed to know a lot about airplanes. "That's the engine starting," she announced when the engines started. "They've closed the doors," she whispered when the doors closed tight. "We're climbing now," she yelled as we gained altitude. Every time I put on the headphones she would tap me on the knee and look me in the eye until I was forced to give up on Mozart and listen to her never-ending soliloquy.

—Peter Davis, "You Don't Choose Your Travel Companions"

The manager looked at me a moment. "The t-shirts are only for the staff," he said finally, as though it was not up to him. He was just reporting the rule. He thought that ended the matter. He was wrong.

"So if you can't sell me a t-shirt," I said slowly, "who can?" I waited, making it clear I wasn't going to give up easily. The manager laughed to himself, looked at his watch, then said something to one of the other guys in

Danish. A brief conversation ensued. Then all three of them looked up at me. The manager said, "The owner is in the club. If you want a t-shirt, you can ask him."

"In the club," I said, making sure. He nodded. I thanked him and went back outside to the door of the club. Once again I knocked loudly on the door and waited a long time. Once again I heard the other guy come up the stairs, take down the chain, unlock the locks, and shoot the bolts. He did not seem surprised to see me.

"I'm supposed to talk to the owner," I said. "Downstairs, in the club."

"You really want this shirt," the guy said. He opened the door wide enough for me to enter. I followed him down the stairs, over to the bar, and then around a corner to an open doorway. The guy pointed toward the doorway and said, "That's the office." Then he went behind the bar. I took a deep breath and stepped into the office of the Jazzhus Montmartre.

It was a small, low-ceilinged, windowless room all but filled with two desks, some shelves, and some filing cabinets. There were faded posters on the walls, and a calendar. Both people in the stuffy little room were talking on the phone. At one desk a woman had a big ledger book open in front of her, and she was talking insistently to whoever was on the other end of the line. She had her back to me.

The owner was at the other desk, talking on another phone. He was a genial-looking guy my father's age. When he hung up his phone and looked at me expectantly, I gathered all my resolve. So rarely in life does one get a travel t-shirt opportunity with real merit, and this was the guy who could make it a reality.

"Good morning," I said. "The manager said I should come down and see you about a t-shirt for my brother."

"The manager sent you?"

"Yes."

"But he made a mistake. We don't sell the shirts."

"But you could," I pointed out.

"They are not for sale," he said.

"But they're yours," I said. "You can do whatever you want with them!"

"No."

"Why not?"

"Because they're only for the staff."

I sagged against the wall. I had gone all the way to the top, and the damn t-shirts were still not for sale. In America, *everything* is for sale. We sell our Hollywood studios to the Japanese, our publishing companies to the Germans, and the names of famous sports stadiums to snack chip companies. Why did these people in Denmark insist on the purity of their t-shirts?

The owner of the club shrugged, his palms upturned in the universal gesture of nonresponsibility. Behind him the woman kept talking on the phone. I pulled myself together and reminded myself that this guy was practically related to me. My grandparents were Danish. He was Danish. He really wanted to sell me a shirt. He just didn't know it.

I explained about my brother, and about listening to Stan Getz records from the Jazzhus Montmartre, and everything. The owner of the club listened impassively. When I finished, he said, "You must be American." I nodded. "But you look Danish. What is your name?"

I told him, pronouncing the family name as Danishly as possible.

"Elkjaer?" the club owner said, surprised. "Like Preban Elkjaer?"

In fact, the family name had been Peterson in Denmark and was changed to the Americanized "Elkjer" for reasons I won't go into here. But I was not about to quibble about things like spelling when I could get a boost from the fact that Denmark's best soccer player had a name that sounded like mine. So I nodded.

"Preban Elkjaer is the most famous footballer in Denmark!" the owner exclaimed. "Everyone in Denmark knows Preban Elkjaer. Are you related to him?"

Now I was on the spot. I didn't want to lie outright, but my travel t-shirt idea hung in the balance. "In America," I said, "anyone called 'Elkjer' is a cousin of ours," I said. I was splitting a geographical hair—it's unlikely that anyone called Elkjaer in Denmark is a cousin of ours—but the statement I had made was, strictly speaking, true. And it worked.

"Well, if we're talking about a relation of Preban Elkjaer," the club owner said with a smile, "I think we can let your brother have a t-shirt from the Jazzhus Montmartre. Now let me find out the price." He leaned over and tapped the woman on the shoulder. She put her hand over the telephone receiver and looked up at him, impatiently.

"This guy is a cousin of Preban Elkjaer," he told her. He came all the way from America to buy a t-shirt from the club. How much would it cost?"

The woman glanced at me, then turned to her boss with a look that said he should know better. "They're only for the staff," she said, and turned back to her phone call.

In the end, I got the shirt, but the club owner had to repeat everything I had said, and throw in some of his own ideas, to convince the woman to name a price. And since they had never sold the shirts, the price she came up with was stiff. I didn't argue. When I got to the top of the stairs, the guy who had let me in saw that I had a shirt. He asked me how much I paid for it. When I told him, he said, "I should have sold you mine."

*Thom Elkjer is a novelist and journalist who has contributed to the Travelers' Tales volumes* Paris, Italy, Food, The Road Within, *and* The Gift of Travel. *He is also the editor of* Adventures in Wine: True Stories of Vineyards and Vintages around the World *and the author of* Escape to the Wine Country *and* Beautiful Wineries. *He lives with his wife, fine art painter Antoinette von Grone, among the vineyards of Anderson Valley in Northern California.*

MARK SALZMAN

# The Rodent

*An American teaching in China becomes a legend. Well, sort of.*

"LET'S LOOK IT UP AND SEE," I SAID TO THE GROUP OF STUDENTS who had visited me to ask about the meaning of an obscure word. No sooner had I picked up my copy of *The American College Dictionary* than I heard one of the girls scream. I looked up and saw them all staring wide-eyed at my desk. A rat had jumped on it and was running around looking, presumably, for a way to jump off. With a great yell I slammed the dictionary down on the table. I had intended only to be funny, but by unfortunate coincidence the rat darted into the path of the dictionary and was annihilated. The students laughed and applauded, saying it was a magnificent demonstration of "real *gong fu*." On the spot they gave me the nickname "*Da Shu Haohan*," Rat-Killing Hero, a play on "*Da Hu Haohan*," Tiger-Killing Hero, the epithet of a legendary warrior. They had a wonderful time reviewing aloud exactly how it had happened and what it had looked and sounded like, so that when they told all their friends the story would be consistent. Eventually, though, something had to be done with the little corpse. I opted for leaving it on my desk as a warning to other rodents, but the students had a better idea: "Teacher Mark, there is a reward for killing rats! Bring it to the Rat Collection Office and you will get a mao (about five cents) for it." So the whole pack of us walked across the campus, with me at the front holding the rat by the tail, and my students behind me holding sheets of paper with the rat's crimes written out on them.

By the time we reached the Rat Collection Office, we had attracted quite a crowd. I explained to the comrade-in-charge where and how I had killed the rat, put it on the table and asked for my reward. He and the other men in the office laughed heartily when they heard the circumstances of the rat's demise, but as the comrade-in-charge went to his desk to take out a mao, one of his colleagues pulled him aside for a brief conversation. Then the comrade-in-charge took a few of my students aside and talked to them for a few minutes.

At last he picked up the rat, tied a string to its tail and walked over to me. "I'm sorry to say that we can't pay you. The regulation is that the reward be given to students who kill rats in the dormitories. But here," he said, handing me the string and smiling, "why don't you take it outside and play with it? When you're done, just throw it away."

I thanked him and left. Outside the building I asked if anyone had any ideas how to play with the rat, but no one did, so I threw it away. When we returned to the Foreign Languages Office, one of the students giggled and asked if I wanted to know why they didn't give me the reward. "Sure—why?" "Because the other comrade pointed out that the official statement concerning rats is that they have been stamped out. Only internal documents, which foreigners can't read, discuss the rat problem. Since you killed the rat, well, there's nothing to be done about that. But if they give you the reward, then an official disburser of state funds will have publicly confirmed to a foreign resident that rats do exist here. They might have been criticized."

I couldn't resist asking the student if he didn't think that was a bit silly. "Oh, of course it is very silly. But the comrades in the office, like anyone else, would rather do something silly than something stupid."

*Mark Salzman began studying Chinese martial arts, calligraphy, and ink painting when he was thirteen. He graduated from Yale in 1982 with a degree in Chinese language and literature. From 1982 to 1984 he lived in China, where he taught English at Hunan Medical College. This story was excerpted from his book* Iron & Silk. *He lives in Los Angeles with his wife, the filmmaker Jessica Yu, and their daughter, Ava.*

*

A loud clank up under the corrugated-iron roof brought me back to full consciousness. With disbelief I remembered exactly where I was—and then someone screamed outside. Something hit the bed and scratched against my arm. Jesus, I thought, sliding sideways and grabbing the torch from the top of the pack. *It's a spear through the shutter.* And I snapped on the light.

From the head of the bed, an enormous, fluffy, white-bellied, gray-backed rat looked at me, frozen, his eyes as wide as mine, his cheeks puffed out, his ears forward, shaped like spoons, his tail white at the end and much too long. We stared at each other, both of us hyperventilating; the fur over his rib cage pumped in and out; my heart twitched like a dislodged ball of maggots in my chest.

"It's O.K.," I said, shaking. "You're a rat."

The rat, appalled by such obviousness in the middle of the night, jumped at the wall, scrabbled, fell off again, and scuttered out of the door.

—Redmond O'Hanlon, *Congo Journey*

Cartoon by Dave Whamond

LYNN FERRIN

# It's a Man's World

*Sometimes nature leaves you hanging.*

A FEW PITCHES UP THE ROYAL ARCHES, WE DECIDED, WOULD make a nice climb on this sultry summer afternoon in Yosemite Valley. We'd be down in time for a leisurely dinner and campfire and schmoozing around Camp Four under the August moon.

Ray was the ideal climbing partner for a novice like me; he hadn't fully recovered from his bone-smashing spill on the ice wall at Nun Kun, and his leg was still in a brace. He still wasn't ready to go back to climbing with the big boys, but he liked keeping his skills honed, and anyway in those days he was one of the few honchos around Camp Four who was willing and nice enough to climb with females.

Now, the Royal Arches are very aesthetic, big curving granite overhangs, like the cloisters of medieval monasteries, on the northeast side of the valley, above The Ahwahnee Hotel. It's a nice walk over there, on the forest path that runs along the bottom of the valley walls.

O.K, so we rope up and Ray leads, placing pins—back

then we were still using pitons. I'd follow and pull them out as I moved up the rock face. Also, instead of modern harnesses, we used just a wrapped-webbing "swami" belt about our waists for tying in. (A bit of background important to this story.)

I always enjoyed those times when it was my turn to belay Ray as he moved up, concentrating hard on the task at hand, but something in my mind always went off wool-gathering. I'd muse about how beautiful the place was, those waterfalls plunging down the silver walls into the wildflowers, and how you can remember one kiss on a ledge longer than you can remember a whole relationship. And how climbers could be such bastards and how the good ones had no footsteps. I mean, you could never hear them approaching. But that's another story.

Anyway, we had done about three pitches, and I was tied in to a bolt and belaying Ray from a very miniscule ledge when I realized I shouldn't have guzzled so much lemonade before we started. When he got to the top of the pitch, I decided, I'd take care of it before I started climbing. He'd be out of sight above, and I couldn't see anyone below right then. But jeez, the ledge was only four inches wide at most, with solid, vertical rock behind it.

I know, I'd let him pull the rope tight and that would hold me in place while I sort of balanced with my toes on the ledge, facing the wall. Got that?

O.K., so he gets to the top of his pitch, yells that he's off belay, and ties himself in to start belaying me. "Ready to climb?" he calls a moment later. "Uh, not quite yet. But I'm on belay. Up rope!"

The rope pulls taut, I turn and face the wall. I yell for him to give me a little slack. So I can get into a comfortable squat, see.

"What are you doing?" he calls.

"Uh, nothing, I'll start in a second. But keep the rope tight." Swami, buttons, zippers, layers of clothes. Gawd. Success! Now then…

"Hey," comes his voice, "whaddaya doing?"

I was almost finished. "Just a minute! I'll come up soon!" For some reason he took that as a command to pull up the rope. It was just enough to knock me off balance.

I fell off the ledge, and swung at the end of my rope, on the wall high above The Ahwahnee Hotel, *flagrante delicto*, so to speak. Then I had to get back on the wall and inch my way up to the ledge from which I'd fallen. Did you ever try to rock climb with your pants around your ankles?

*Lynn Ferrin says that "even though the hardware has changed enormously since she was rock-climbing in the early '70s, women still have the same software problem." Ferrin, who lives and writes in San Francisco, has pressed her boots against most of the world's great mountain ranges, from the Himalayas to the Alps to the Andes, but her heart has always belonged to the magic, mystery, and beauty of Yosemite.*

*

Seems God was just about done creating the universe, but he had two extra things left in his bag of creations, so he decided to split them between Adam and Eve.

He told the couple that one of the things he had to give away was the ability to stand up while urinating. "It's a handy thing," God told the couple, "I was wondering if either one of you wanted that very ability."

Adam jumped up and blurted, "Oh, give that one to me! I'd love to be able to do that! It seems a sort of thing a man should do. Oh please, oh please, oh please, let me have that ability. It'd be so great! When I'm working in the garden or naming the animals, I could just stand there and let it fly. It'd be so cool, I could write my name in the sand. Oh please, God, let it be me who you give that gift to, let me stand and pee, oh please...." On and on he went like an excited little boy who had to pee.

Eve just smiled and told God that if Adam really wanted it so badly, that he should have it. It seemed to be the sort of thing that would make him happy, and she really wouldn't mind if Adam were the one given this ability.

And so Adam was given the ability to urinate while in a vertical position. He was happy and did celebrate by wetting down the bark on the tree nearest him, laughing with delight all the while.

"Fine," God said looking back into his bag of leftovers, "What's left here? Oh yes, multiple orgasms...."

—Anonymous

ROLF POTTS

* * *

# Penny Pinched

*Outsmarting the locals was his game.*

SINCE IT'S ALWAYS NICE TO BLAME SOMEONE ELSE FOR YOUR own folly, I am tempted to recast Chad as a seedy caricature: a hustler or a pimp; a greasy loser with feathered hair and a pinky ring; a sniggering reject who was always making obnoxious noises with his armpits or asking me to smell his finger.

But in reality, Chad was an earnest, mostly harmless Canadian backpacker who was only trying to be helpful.

"Where are you headed?" he'd asked me when I first met him. Since we were taking the Chao Phraya river ferry through Bangkok, this seemed to me like a perfectly legitimate conversation-starter.

"The train station," I'd told him. "I'm going up to Phitsanulok for the night. It's a good midway point to Chiang Mai, and I hear they have a great youth hostel there."

"Yeah, the hostel in Phitsanulok is as good as you'll find anywhere. Free toast and coffee in the mornings. Just be careful with the *tuk-tuk* drivers at the train station."

"*Tuk-tuk* drivers?"

"Yeah, they're all a bunch of hard-asses. If you're a Westerner, they won't take you anywhere for under 100 baht. You're better to just get off the train one stop early and walk to the youth hostel. Save you a lot of money."

In retrospect, I suppose I could have kept things simple and brushed off Chad's advice. After all, 100 baht amounts to less than $3. But for a budget traveler such as myself, an insider's tip on how to save any amount of money is a forbidden fruit too tempting to leave hanging. When I got to the Bangkok station, I discovered that the entire six-hour train trip to Phitsanulok cost only 109 baht, third-class. Reasoning that it would be foolish to pay another 100 baht for a mere five-minute *tuk-tuk* trip to the youth hostel, I resolved to take Chad's advice when I arrived at my destination.

Despite a few petty discomforts, riding the third-class train is a wonderful way to experience Thailand. Unlike the pressure-sealed sterility of first-class, third-class allows you to roll down the windows—to stick your head out and squint into the wind, to smell the countryside, to barter for ice cream and fresh pineapple at the stations. The route to Phitsanulok transports the rider past the crumbling stupas of Ayutthaya, the monkey-infested shrines of Lop Buri and the late-day glitter of the glass-mirrored temples outside of Nakhon Sawan. During the dry season, the plains of central Thailand are aglow with stubble fires, and sudden plumes of smoke swirl through the train cars like ghosts.

I was not bored once during the six-hour trip. South of Ayutthaya, a trio of blue-uniformed high school girls handed me chunks of jackfruit as they practiced their English ("What is your hobby?" "Can you do dancing?" "Do you think you're handsome?"). Past Lop Buri, a gregarious country grandmother babbled in Thai as she nonchalantly rifled through the contents of my day pack; when she'd seen enough, she unceremoniously presented me with a Buddhist amulet. Later, when I moved up to the dining car to eat fried rice and look out at the stars, a middle-aged Thai man seized my phrase book and engaged me in inexplicable English small talk for the entire duration of my meal. "Is this the post office?" he would bellow proudly, not bothering to wait for a reply. "Can you wash these clothes?"

By the time I was due for my strategic early exit from the third-class coach, I was downright euphoric. "First-class travel," I sagely declared to myself, "is a state of mind."

When the conductor informed me that Bang Krathum was the last stop before Phitsanulok, I was so confident of my good fortune that I didn't even bother to double-check Chad's fabled shortcut to the youth hostel. Had I taken a few moments to do so, I would have discovered that there's a critical scheduling difference between local trains and incoming trains from Bangkok.

Oblivious to this distinction, I walked along the frontage road that ran out from Bang Krathum station. A group of teenagers coasted up behind me on bicycles.

"Where you go?" one boy asked as he pedaled by.

"Phitsanulok," I said.

"Ha ha ha!" the group replied in unison.

Unfortunately, laughter is not an internationally standardized form of communication. At the time, I took it to mean, "This clever foreigner knows about the shortcut to the youth hostel!" Even when the youth hostel didn't materialize after five, fifteen, thirty minutes—the merry mask of optimism kept me going.

It wasn't until I stumbled into a mosquito-infested boondock called Mae Thiap one hour later that I reconsidered the laughter. Perhaps it had meant something more along the lines of "This foreigner has obviously been smoking crack!"

Fortunately for me, the one person awake in Mae Thiap at that time of night happened to speak a bit of English.

"Where you go?" asked a stocky, mustachioed man, who sat on the stoop of his house sipping a tall bottle of Singha beer.

"Phitsanulok," I said.

Mr. Mustache raised a skeptical eyebrow. "Phitsanulok is very far."

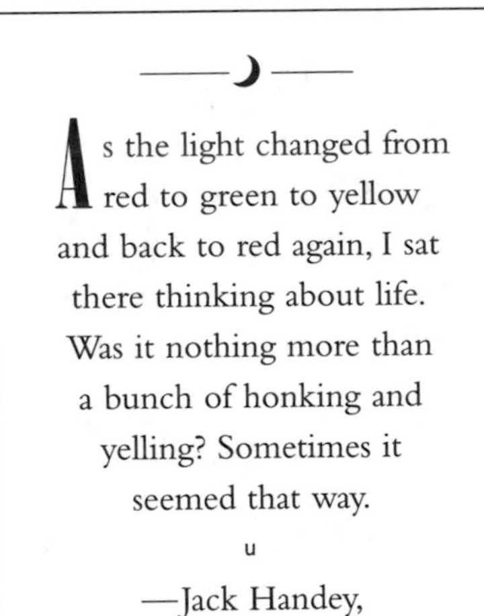

As the light changed from red to green to yellow and back to red again, I sat there thinking about life. Was it nothing more than a bunch of honking and yelling? Sometimes it seemed that way.

—Jack Handey, *Deeper Thoughts: All New, All Crispy*

"No," I said, somewhat desperately. As if to illustrate, I made two fists. "Bang Krathum station, Phitsanulok station." I put my fists together to show how close, presumably, these two places were to each other.

Mr. Mustache shook his head, set down his beer bottle, and held up his fists. "Bang Krathum, Mae Thiap."

"Yes!" I exclaimed. "Bang Krathum, Mae Thiap, Phitsanulok." Optimistically, I made the proper hand gestures.

"Ha ha ha!" said Mr. Mustache. He made an exaggerated flurry of fist gestures, looking vaguely like a background dancer from that old Nancy Sinatra video. I began to wonder if he was drunk.

"Bang Krathum, Mae Thiap," he said. "Ban Mai, Bung Phra, Phitsanulok."

I felt a hollow tickle in my stomach: I was still two stations away from my shortcut. At this rate, it would be dawn before I got to the youth hostel. As if reading my mind, Mr. Mustache stood up. "Let's go Phitsanulok," he said. He walked around to the side of his house and wheeled out a battered off-road motorcycle. "Three hundred baht," he said, suddenly businesslike.

At this point, I realized that Mr. Mustache had me in a pinch. Nobody else was awake in Mae Thiap, and I wasn't about to trudge the hour back to Bang Krathum. Had he demanded that I pay for the ride with my spare kidney, I would have been forced to give it serious consideration.

Still, since I was technically in the process of saving 100 baht, I decided to try to talk him down. "One hundred fifty baht," I said.

Mr. Mustache grinned. "Three hundred baht."

Resisting the urge to swat at the mosquitoes that were dive-bombing my ears, I looked him in the eye. "Two hundred baht."

"Ha ha ha!" Mr. Mustache said. "Three hundred baht."

After another couple minutes of this, we finally agreed on an arrangement that allowed me to maintain a thin shred of self-esteem: 300 baht, but I got to wear the helmet.

It took us forty-five minutes to get to Phitsanulok, but I think Mr. Mustache got lost a couple times. By the time we pulled into the train station—the very place I had spent all this effort trying to avoid—it was after midnight. My eyes felt like they were crusted with dead insects.

"Where you go?" asked a station *tuk-tuk* driver. Avoiding his eyes, I hurried off down the street. I had no idea where the youth hostel was in relation to the main train station, but at that moment I really didn't care. On principle, taking a *tuk-tuk* was out of the question.

One block from the train station, a chubby middle-aged woman pulled her moped over to me.

"You wan' go to hotel?" she asked. Despite her age and somewhat homely appearance, there was a certain verve to the way she talked. Thankful for the presumed gesture of kindness, I climbed onto the back of her moped. I absently noted she was wearing a short-skirted 1970s-soft-porn chambermaid's uniform. I was too tired to think this strange at the time.

"I'm staying at the youth hostel," I told her.

"You hotel?"

"Youth hostel."

"You want lady?"

Not prepared for this sort of non sequitur, I said nothing. As if to emphasize her point, Moped Woman leaned back and nuzzled my cheek with hers. I held on to the moped seat in shock: imagine Benjamin Braddock being seduced not by Mrs. Robinson, but by a matronly pipe-organist from the Methodist Women's Missionary League.

"No lady!" I said, recovering. "I want sleep."

"Lady! Lady!" Moped Woman exclaimed. Suddenly, she reached back and gave my crotch a squeeze. "Lady!"

"Sleep!" I yelled. "No lady!"

Something was wrong in the way she grabbed at me. Somehow, her hand was too powerful, her grip too knowing. I nearly fell off the moped trying to slap her arm away.

Sulkily, Moped Woman dropped me off at the parking lot of the Thani Hotel. One good look at her face confirmed my suspicion: Moped Woman was Moped Man.

I had heard of the *katoey*—the Thai transvestite "lady-boy"—before, but for some reason I thought *katoeys* were supposed to look like Diana Ross, Wonder Woman, or Cher. Moped Lady looked more like Alice from *The Brady Bunch*.

"You give me 100 baht," she demanded as I turned to leave.

By this point, the only way anyone could have convinced me to cough up 100 baht would be if it somehow included snapping Chad's trachea with my bare hands. One hundred baht had become a watermark, a line in the sand, a mirror that reflected the painful emptiness of my own soul. I gave Moped Woman 50 baht and fled, above her angry protestations, into the Thani Hotel.

When Moped Lady was still skulking around the parking lot after twenty minutes, I resigned myself to a night in the polished high-class confines of the Thani. The only room available cost 1,200 baht.

Minus the 80 baht it would have cost me to stay at the youth hostel, saving 100 baht on a *tuk-tuk* ride had ended up costing me a grand total of 1,470 baht.

The following morning's complimentary breakfast buffet at the Thani was so zealously air-conditioned that my bacon and eggs were cold by the time I got them back to my table. Noting my presence, the hotel staff abruptly yanked the ambient Thai music from the sound system, replaced it with a Scorpions album and cranked the volume to full blast. By the time "Rock You Like a Hurricane" had hit its second chorus, I had abandoned my eggs, gathered my pack and hoofed it halfway across the parking lot.

Twenty-five meters later, I stumbled across the youth hostel. There, in the garden courtyard, an international group of backpackers blissfully sipped coffee, munched toast, and listened to Vivaldi. I checked in without further hesitation.

My stay at the youth hostel, I am happy to report, was completely uneventful. The only detail of note was a friendly warning from an English backpacker as I checked out the next morning.

"Watch out for those *tuk-tuk* drivers," she said, noting that I was preparing to head for the train station. "If you're a Westerner, they won't take you anywhere for less than 50 baht."

If she had any advice on how to get around paying that 50 baht, I didn't wait around to hear it.

*Rolf Potts is the author of* Vagabonding: An Uncommon Guide to the Art of Long-Term World Travel. *The former Salon.com columnist is best known for promoting the ethic of vagabonding—a way of living that makes extended, personally meaningful travel possible. His work has appeared in* National Geographic Adventure, National Geographic Traveler, The Best American Travel Writing, The Best Travel Writing, *and on National Public Radio. Visit his website at www.rolfpotts.com.*

⁕

Many languages in Asia are tonal. By adding a different inflection, or tone to the same sound, it changes the meaning. Mandarin has four tones, Vietnamese seven. A young Vietnamese man attempted to teach me how to say, "No MSG please." He held his tact as long as possible, then busted a gut. The vocabulary was easy enough but apparently my English mouth was programmed to hit the tone to request "No boils on my ass, please."

—Jim Soliski, "Does Your Meter Work?"

Cartoon by Benita Epstein

JOHN FLINN

* * *

# Called on the Carpet in Marrakech

*Don't leave home without your Wile E. Coyote moves.*

SOMEBODY WITH MORE EXPERIENCE IN THESE THINGS THAN I once warned that every glass of "free" mint tea you drink in a Moroccan carpet shop ends up costing you $600.

I remembered this with a shudder as I finished my second glass. My new friend, Mohammed, and I were already forty-five minutes into what was shaping up as monumental battle of wills. Moroccan carpet sellers like Mohammed are justly renowned as the world's most skilled and persuasive salesmen. And I had absolutely, positively no intention of walking out of his shop with a carpet.

So, what was I doing there? One of the salient, unassailable facts of travel in Morocco is that sooner or later—usually sooner—you're going to end up in a carpet shop, like it or not. Every local guide, tout, taxi driver, and hotel employee is part of a baksheesh-fueled conspiracy to steer you into the shops. As it turned out, several people in my tour group wanted to shop for carpets, so there was no avoiding at least ducking my head in.

We stepped out of the baking Marrakesh sun into the cool, tiled, palacelike interior of one grand shop. Dazzling, colorful Berber carpets hung from every wall; the wooden beams of the ceiling were carved exquisitely.

"I'm going to poke around the neighborhood," I told our guide. "I'll meet you back here in an hour, O.K.?"

Before I could escape, the door was blocked by a short Moroccan man holding a tray filled with glasses of sweet mint tea.

"Please," said Mohammed, an impeccably dressed salesman who had just materialized at my side. "Before you go, have some tea. Come. Please. Sit."

"Thanks, but I'm not interested in buying a carpet today."

"Just looking," Mohammed said, flashing a gold-toothed smile. "Looking is free. Please. Sit."

"Seriously. I'm not buying anything."

"Of course, of course. Now, please—come, sit. Tell me, where do you come from?"

"California."

Mohammed recoiled with surprise and delight. The coincidence was too much to bear.

"California!? I am a friend of California! I have a cousin in California! Perhaps you would like to meet him sometime?" As we sat down, Mohammed told me he had another cousin who moved to Las Vegas for a year and made so much money selling used cars he was now comfortably retired in Fez. I didn't find this hard to believe.

Mohammed snapped his fingers, and as I sipped my tea an attendant began, with considerable flourish, to unroll carpets at my feet. They were lustrous, intricate, and so beautiful I couldn't imagine walking on them. Mohammed nudged me, lowered his voice, and looked around conspiratorially.

"These are beautiful, yes? You like? They come from my cousin's village in the High Atlas Mountains. For you, I can get special price."

"No need for that. I'm really not in the market to buy anything today," I said, putting down my empty glass. "Thanks for your time. I'm going to go walk around the neighborhood."

Before I could get up, one attendant was handing me a second glass of tea and another was unfurling a new series of carpets.

"I understand, I understand," said Mohammed, putting his hand gently on my arm. "I can see you are a real connoisseur of carpets. Please, look. These are my special carpets. Beautiful, no? What color do you like?"

I wasn't going any farther down this path.

"Periwinkle," I said flatly. "Now, I'd really like to go."

This fazed Mohammed for a moment, but he rebounded nicely.

"We have no periwin-

---

When the English-speaking Mohamid cha-cha'd into the room with all the dramatics of an overacted stage play and poured me a second glass of mint tea, I was ready to tell him not to launch into any sales pitches. I never got the chance. Forty-five minutes may have passed, but I can't be sure, of Mohamid waving his body back and forth, his eyes never averting from mine. I sat transfixed, hypnotized, moving in time to his rhythm. Pots of mint tea kept coming from other rooms while Mohamid entranced me with carpet yarns. At some point, I recall babbling, "Carpets, carpets, yes, I want carpets...carpets...."

—Laurie Gough, *Kite Strings of the Southern Cross*

kle. You like red, yes? Red is very beautiful. Now, how large is your living room."

"It is the size of a postage stamp."

"You are having fun with me, yes? Please: what size carpet do you like?"

"I told you: I don't want any size carpet. I'm leaving now."

"How big is your family room."

"The size of a postcard."

"And your bedroom?"

"The size of a ten-dirham note."

As the attendant finished rolling out yet another batch of samples, we sat staring at a pile that had grown to nearly three feet.

Mohammed tried another tack.

"Which do you like best?"

"They're all beautiful, Mohammed, but, like I told you: I'm not buying any."

"But which do you like best?"

"Why does it matter if I'm not buying one?"

"Please. Which do you like?"

"All right," I said, wondering which of us was going to exhaust the other's patience first. "The one on the very bottom."

Wearily, the attendant began to roll up the several dozen carpets on top of it.

"Very good choice," said Mohammed. "I can see you are a man who knows carpets. So…how much you give me for this one?"

"Nothing, because I'm not buying it."

By now the others in my group had finished their negotiations, purchased their carpets, and were standing near the door, giving me let's-get-going looks.

"How much?" repeated Mohammed.

"I changed my mind," I said, turning and pointing to the far wall. "I think I like that one way over there."

Mohammed turned to look, but by the time he looked back to me it was too late. I was already three steps toward the door and gaining speed.

*John Flinn is executive travel editor of the* San Francisco Chronicle. *He lives in the often-foggy coastal town of Pacifica, south of San Francisco.*

⋆

Love it or hate it, baksheesh is a way of life in Egypt. Almost everyone wants largesse in exchange for a service, even one as small as turning on a wash-room tap. And, everyone has a favorite story.

My award for sheer gall goes to an old guy hanging around the Pyramids, who mooched a cigarette off me...then demanded baksheesh in return for lighting mine! But, as a practitioner of the art, he's left a country mile behind by the mounted policeman I met at the Citadel.

Sitting on a beautiful white horse, sternly moustached, dressed in immaculate whites, and caparisoned in *aiguillettes* and shining black leather, he was a picture waiting to be taken. "*Moomkin surah?*" (May I take a picture?) I asked. "*Inshallah!*" said the magnificent representative of Cairo's Finest, nodding in agreement.

God was indeed willing; I took my pictures and felt in my pocket for a small note for the customary "model fee." "No! No!" said the policeman, shaking his head. "Policemans must not take baksheesh!" Then he reached down, took the note and grinned. "Horse can take baksheesh!!"

—Keith Kellett, "Baksheesh"

GARY A. WARNER

# Passing the Test in Silverton

*It measures an important kind of intelligence.*

SO THERE I'M STANDING IN A PUB IN THE OUTBACK OF Australia with a bright red funnel down my shorts, a rock on my forehead, and my hands behind my back.

I should have seen it coming. I should have known I was had. But I didn't. Mr. World Traveler, sage adviser to millions, was doomed to play the bumpkin once again.

I'd come to the postapocalyptic Down Under landscape on a crucial mission: to take pictures of a three-legged dog named Jake who hangs out begging for scraps of beef jerky at a bar at the end of a godforsaken road.

The tripod canine is the star attraction at the Silverton Hotel, one of the last classic Outback pubs. They—Jake and the pub—sit at the far end of a nearly deserted mining town on the edge of the vast, dry Mundi Mundi Plain.

The train to Silverton closed down a few years back, so to get to Jake, I needed wheels. The nearest rental car agency was a half hour away in Broken Hill.

The manager explains that she is all out of Land Rovers,

Jeeps, and other manly Outback-type vehicles. All she has left is a big wedding-cake-white Ford four-door sedan usually rented out for marriage ceremonies. I slap down the credit card and zoom down the two-lane in the Nuptialmobile.

"How can we dance when our earth is turning. How can we sleep while our beds are burning." The socialist screech of Midnight Oil's Peter Garrett demanding justice for the Aborigines plays in my head—the only place it can play, since the tape deck on the wedding sedan is busted.

I blast the air conditioning and wheel out, gravel spitting from beneath the four fat radials.

The road out to Silverton is a long, lumpy blacktop called the "Mad Max Highway" because it's where they filmed one of the *Road Warrior* movies in which Mel Gibson puts on leathers, drives around very fast, and kills people. This was long before his later hit movie *Braveheart*, in which he puts on a kilt, runs around very fast, and kills people. For that he won an Academy Award.

About five miles out of town, I catch some movement out of the corner of my eye. One, two, three kangaroos, bounding alongside the road. Hares dart out in front of my car, racing across the road.

One—a big gray—didn't make it. THUMP-THUMP. Roadkill in the rearview mirror. Sizing up the huge "roos," I hope none of them ambles into my lane, or it might be me splayed out on the two-lane.

In the seat next to me is Mike-the-Photographer, a sunburned Crocodile Dundee look-alike who peppers his conversation with words like "aperture" and "f-stop" when he's not rooting around in his big black bag full of lenses and gizmos. He's got a worried look on his bright-pink, sunburned brow.

"I hope the light gets soft," he says, referring to the blazing sphere of life as if it were a seersucker shirt in a Downy commercial.

As we whizz by the Dreamland Mine, the Australian Outback steams at 100 degrees outside the windows of our air-conditioned Ford, the bleak rock-and-dust landscape stretching up toward the horizon.

Pulling into the Silverton Hotel's gravel lot, Mike is crestfallen. "Damn, morning light—it's going to be backlit," he says.

I nod knowingly, but am relieved when Mike explains anyway—the pub faces east, meaning the "good light" will be in the morning. The afternoon light means Mike would have to shoot directly into the sun.

"Maybe if we hang out awhile, I can work something," he says.

Hanging out "awhile" in photographer parlance means several hours.

That's problematic in Silverton, a destination short on your usual tourism options. What's left of the town is a collection of abandoned buildings and gum trees. One old church had been converted into an artist's studio with a half-buried psychedelic Volkswagon out front. But it's closed.

Trudging along a dirt road, we meet resident Scott Lennon and ask him what locals do to kill time.

"It's as hot as Hades and you just have to stay out of the midday sun and drink a lot of cold beer," he says.

Blessed with the local wisdom, we head over to the Silverton Hotel, where Jake is using his best hangdog expression in hopes that grizzled pub denizens will toss him a chunk of their beefy snacks.

Innkeeper Ines McLeod is finishing her ironing behind the

bar, then saunters over to pour us a couple of Castlemaine XXXX beers.

Soon we're on our third round, watching the Australian version of *The Price Is Right* on television.

Host: "The tree under which the jolly swagman sat in 'Waltzing Matilda.'"

Crusty Guy #1: "Coolabah."

Host: "Bird that sits in the gum tree in the popular song."

Crusty Guy #1: "Kookaburra."

"Some sheila," Crusty Guy #2 elbows his friend, winking toward the Australian version of Vanna White turning the letters.

Banjo, a muscular purebred Australian cattle dog, comes out from behind the bar to mooch a piece of my chili beef jerky. A long stick is gone in a single chomp. My largesse attracts Jake, who rouses from his woolly lair to amble over to get his share.

"Nothing for Jake—he's on a diet," Ines warns.

I scratch him behind the ear, and he wiggles his stub up and down in joy.

"Ines, another beer, please," I ask.

"Just a sec, mate—one last shirt," she says. Jake tries to mesmerize me into forking over the jerky, so I get up and wander around the tiny bar, looking at the photographs of celebrities on the wall. There's Mel Gibson. Nicole Kidman. And an awful lot of famous Australian people I've never heard of.

In one corner is a list. "Passed The Test" it says. Mel's on the list. So's Nicole.

"What's the test?" I ask Ines.

"Oh, just something we do when we get a crowd in here," she says, cleaning up some stray beer "tinnies" on one end of the bar.

"How does it work?" I press in my best slightly inebriated attack journalist mode.

"Everybody lines up at the bar," she says. "You stick a funnel in your pants. Then you lean back and balance a rock on your forehead, put one hand on the bar and the other behind your back. The first one who can successfully roll the rock into the funnel wins a free beer. People are pretty drunk, so it usually takes a few tries to get a winner."

"Let's do it," I say to Mike. He's game. After all, it's still an hour to "soft light."

We line up at the bar. Ines hands us the funnels. A couple of grinning local boys stop watching TV and come over to watch the race. Jake saunters by to catch the action.

We put the funnels in our pants. The rocks on our foreheads. One hand on the bar. The other behind. Concentration is the key to the game.

"O.K.," Ines says. "Get ready. On the count of three. One...two..."

Suddenly there's a piercing wet cold in my underwear. The regulars burst into laughter. Jake barks.

Ines has poured a glass of ice water into our funnels. The fronts of our pants look unmistakably like we've just experienced a Richter-scale bladder control failure.

"You passed the test," Ines shouts. "Here's your free beer." She reaches behind the bar for a thimble-sized glass filled with flat Fosters lager.

"You got us," I say feebly. Mike gives me one of those pained "thanks-for-getting-me-into-this" looks, and we turn to walk out of the bar. We walk outside where a small knot of locals spy our wet spots, point and smile. Another couple of fools who've been had by Ines.

A desert breeze chills my front side. I squint toward the

west where the sun hangs low—"soft light." Time for the Funnel Warriors to get to work, wearing our passing marks on "The Test" for all to see.

*Gary A. Warner is travel editor of the* Orange County Register.

*

For room service with a difference the award must surely go to the Bark Hut Inn on the Arnhem Highway in the Northern Territory of Australia. I'd spent the day in the bush photographing with a documentary film crew. I wanted to leave my camera gear in the room and have a shower before tucking into a solid NT meal. "The rooms only lock from the inside," the bar girl told me when I asked about security. Then she added, "We've just finished reno vating them," as if these two facts were somehow related.

I drove to my cabin and attempted to open the door. It was locked. Assuming there must be someone in there I knocked and waited. Nothing happened. Assuming that whoever was in there could be sleeping off an NT stupor, I drove back to the bar and informed the young woman of my dilemma. "I'll send the manager," she said.

Once more I drove back to my room. A six-foot-something bloke wearing stubby shorts and sporting tree stumps for legs introduced himself as the manager. "She's locked, mate," he said after trying the door. "Yes, but I was told they only lock from the inside. There must be somebody in there," I replied. Without a word the manager took a few paces back, paused for a second, and then ran furiously toward the door raising his massive work boots to the handle.

The door flew open, the handle flew off and the window at the other end almost blew out. The room was empty. "She's open now," said the manager. That's what I call service.

—Peter Davis, "Room Checking"

"IF YOU HIT THE ROAD, I BELIEVE YOU WOULD BE TAKING A STEP IN THE RIGHT DIRECTION."

Cartoon by Frank Cotham

J. P. DONLEAVY

# The Fox Hunt

*Tallyho! Into the bush they go.*

IN IRELAND, A LAND LONG DOMINATED BY THE INVADER, THE habit of lying has become firmly established. And as a traveler on the road asking a direction you'd be forewarned not to believe everything you hear as to getting to your destination. But by God at the same time you'd come across an honesty right for two these days in a nation now going madly modern out of its mind, exposed as it is to the round-the-clock new social and sexual freedoms broadcast from abroad down out of the skies. Where once only God with his brogue was speaking up there.

Now in the latter case of your concupiscence, here's a type of little story of not that long ago of what you might now expect to confront you in the land of saints and scholars and which erupts as such occasionally does among your missed semiprofessional classes pretending to profess a certain amount of broadminded permissiveness. You'd have, coming as you do, and with some frequency, from England and the USA, damsels easy of virtue and wily in the ways of flattering men to the point of forcing them to sit down immediately to hide the embarrassment of their erections. Now this nature of lady would have her skintight wardrobe and diaphanous garments to fit any occasion, and maybe in extreme cases even her own sports car so as to be seen wearing her haute couture snug arsed-clinging short skirt as she got in and out of her racy vehicle. And in so doing be inciting the appetites of every red-blooded Irishman within whose long repressed sight she came. And by God would some of the less religious of them be apoplectically panting and totally indifferent to the Bedouin atmosphere of every man's breeches looking like a tent. Nor would she be very much concerned taking notice of the glowering Irish women who would watch her lead the men away. Of course, let it be said, not perhaps for decency's sake, but for the geometric difficulties that might be in it, your newcomer seductress would only be taking on one man at a time.

Now we must not confuse this incident about to be told with the more common and accepted occasion when in Ireland saucy shenanigans occur during the likely time of the fox hunt when the blood's up and the hooves are pounding over the turf. It is well known that, with the huntsman's horn sounding, and the hounds giving tongue and the blood lust occasioned by the fox desperately attempting to escape with its life, that this is exactly the time when your interloping foreign lady, her breeches tight over the arse and thighs straining locked over the ribs of her mount leads a likely gent off to the side, well away from the line of the fox. And there dismounted in a sheltered glade, bottoms al fresco do be bouncing. Now this kind of congress is fully understood to happen when members of the opposite sex of the hunt, roused out of their normally private inhibitions, will have at each other in a singularly sexual way with pairs of them flagrantly in copses all over the countryside pounding on top of each other goodo. No, this is not what we are referring to here at all. And in the present situation about to be related, it's all suburban types and cars and not a horse in sight.

Now as we universally know, it's the rich what gets the pleasure, it's the poor what gets the pain. And in Ireland it's long been the case that outside fox hunting circles, it's the natives get the celibacy and the visitor who more often gets the hanky-panky. However, recently in this relatively new nation it has been increasingly your affluent professional business folk who are getting their fair share of licentious shenanigans. And who do in their present lifestyles have champagne delivered to the door of a morning with the milk. And who can, out of the blue, get laid at your company picnics. Especially when a vicar's daughter straight from England shows up and is conversationally everywhere boasting of her multiple orgasms as if she were the only one on the face of the earth so singularly blessed. In any event she wasn't shy in letting it be known that she, given the appropriate Irishman, was ready and willing for a gallop. A nice enough and friendly and generous girl she was. Who'd give you a wondrous smile with the great set of teeth she had gleaming in her head. And arriving in a tight red outfit at the business picnic, didn't she with her plunging neckline soon disappear in what was the early twilight of the afternoon and go off with your genuine homegrown exhilarated Irishman to a nearby glade. Now let me tell you there's little or nothing incognito, confidential, or unrevealed in this land, and the pair of them would be watched going by more eyes than you could imagine could be in the thirty-seven or so heads present. And all but one relishing what was about to unfold.

And so, begob, the scene was set. Accumulating in the nearby bushes and shrubberies was a small crowd waiting in peaceful silence as the pair of intending lovers had already unlawfully presented themselves to each other without clothes and were exposing mammary, urinary, and excretory organs contrary to standards of public decency. And it wasn't long before the observing little gathering were waiting clucking their mouths at the gymnastic sexual shenanigans taking place before their very eyes and imported free of custom duty by a member of the British, leisured, upper middle class. Of course in spite of the wrenched, twisted, and trampled foliage, not everything going on between the carnal collaborators could be seen through the leafy undergrowth. But enough to know that their legs were entwined around each other's necks and their heads attending to each other's bifurcations. There was even to be witnessed a little bit of your imported English bondage. Didn't your seductress ask your man to tether her wrists and ankles across her bottom with her belt. And who should now at that very moment of the strap landing, suddenly choose to join this little group of voyeurs but your man's furiously enraged Irish wife.

Now, amazingly, because of the revered Saint Bridget, goddess of fertility, the Irish believe it can bring a curse upon you for interrupting sexual intercourse. So there is no ranting and raving and screaming, "Stop doing that to my husband." And in silence the wife furiously fumed there, as the seductress, stung into action by her chastisement, was loose once more from her restraint and had got up on her supine husband to gyrate like a spinning top teetering in the last of its revolutions. However, it was known at the picnic that this lady seducer so presently busily nakedly entwined, came in her own low-slung motor vehicle that she managed to recently purchase brand-new with money she got out of her last divorced husband. And wasn't it on its four innocent extra-wide wheels, parked not that far away. So didn't some of the ladies of the voyeuristic gang in the bushes steal away while the rest continued watching with patient interest as your lithe seductress assumed a lady dog position and wagging her arse had now your man up on her from behind pumping away like a steam locomotive piston. And busy as both of them were, neither gave any notice to events happening less than fifty yards away. For let me tell you it's one thing in Ireland to quietly and in the customary manner copulate but quite another when you get up to masochistic bondage, gymnastic gyrations, and canine machinations. All of which add fuel to the fury of these Irish women of the group now volunteering to avenge the outrage perpetrated upon this temporarily, as it were, deserted wife. Now you'd feel sorry for the poor spouse whose husband is having a jolly dickens of an old time enjoying himself with this self-proclaimed multiorgasmic vicar's daughter. Don't worry, comeuppance is coming. And there they all are now, already ganged up on the fancy fucking seductress's motorcar. And a shiny, brilliant red it is too.

If your sensibilities are tender towards your beautiful mechanical equipage, don't watch or listen to what is happening next. Splat. That was a massive cake of gravelly mud flung two handedly on the gleaming bonnet. Crash. That was a large stone just thrown through the windscreen. Smash. That latter reverberation was a big red-brown brick you just heard go through the aerodynamically sloped rear window. Boom, boom, boom. Those are boulders heaved pockmarking your deep and sundry dents all over the car roof and body. And the hiss you hear is the air coming out of every last one of the tires and not sparing the spare one. Plus the gang of lady avengers have just twisted off the outside rear-view mirrors specially provided on the front fenders. And through the smashed side windows, they are now able to open up the vehicle's previously locked doors. Having gained access to the perfumed interior, honey from the picnic baskets is now being poured over the cowhide upholstery. And generous fistfuls of butter are being rubbed over any of the honey-free spots remaining. All those colored wires you see pulled out were once connected to the ignition and wrapped colorfully around the gear shift, only God knows what they are connected to now. But one of your men is presently crying out that there's no sugar left for tea. And he's right. Every last bit of it has been poured down into the vicar's daughter's petrol tank, which rumor has it, is guaranteed not to improve the efficiency of the reputed 300 horsepower or thereabouts of this racy vehicle one little bit, and they might as well have dropped a two-ton boulder or two from a far height on top of the engine. Now as the guilty, recently copulating couple, dressed now, innocently wander back to the picnic site licking their chops, you'd wonder why these clannish Irish women instead of systematically destroying the seductress's motorcar, couldn't have been a little more sophisticatedly urbane and simply have made a few of your more pointed remarks reeking of innuendo which would have allowed your seductress to get on her way to other conquests instead of being comforted by your man as she stands there at the side of her Ferrari, head in her hands, sobbing uncontrollably.

*J. P. Donleavy was born in New York City in 1926 and educated there. Following service in the U.S. Navy in World War II, he attended Trinity College, Dublin, and remained in Ireland between 1946 and 1951, finally returning in 1969. Author of some fourteen books, including* The Ginger Man, The Beastly Beatitudes of Balthazar B., *and* A Singular Man, *he is also a highly regarded painter, playwright, and script writer. He is featured in the film* J.P Donleavy's Ireland. *Donleavy lives in a historic mansion near Mullingar in County Westmeath, about 50 miles from Dublin. Busy with farming as well as writing, he reads but does not reply to fan mail. This story was excerpted from his book* A Singular Country.

⁎

"What's a count?" I once asked my mother and my granny and my Aunty Peggy after school.

"A what?"

"A big boy at school called me a count and a bullock."

There was no immediate response, but my father must have been consulted and soon the response came back.

"Your daddy says those are not nice words."

—John Kelly, *Cool About the Ankles*

CARA TABACHNICK

# The Reluctant Chef and Her Rainbow Special

*What's in that soup?*

IT HAD BEEN THREE MONTHS SINCE I'D WASHED MY HAIR, two months since my underwear got stolen off the laundry line, and six days since I last changed my outfit, so I felt sufficiently ready to attend my first Rainbow Gathering/Full Moon Party. It was to take place on the shores of Lago Atitlán in Guatemala. We were looking for Bob's tepee somewhere between San Pedro and Santiago. A favorite gringo hideout, it didn't take long to secure a boat at an astronomical price. As we approached the spot a giant tepee with leaping figures dancing around were visible in the setting sun. Our friendly boatman's face quickly changed to disapproval.

"Gringos," he muttered as he paddled into the dock.

Appropriately insulted, my friend and I jumped out amid screams of "Sister, Sister, welcome!" Strange I mused, I thought my sisters were back in the United States. Soon enough I realized this was the traditional way of greeting in Rainbow Land. Since I didn't have dreadlocks and couldn't name one communal van I'd lived in, I sat on the side watching the festivities.

It was nothing like I'd seen before, and I'd been in Central America a long time. About sixty people were dancing around to the beat of twenty people drumming, singing chants they all seemed to know. Some people were making out, others were spinning around, and the rest were running around naked. Restless, I looked around for someone to make out with since naked running and spinning were out of the question.

That is when I was caught and enlisted to help the kitchen workers whip up a vegan dream for eighty hungry hippies. In a way I was glad; nothing makes me happier than slaving over an open fire at a party. There was a group of about eight of us and with our limited choices we dreamed up a menu of pasta. (I never said we were creative.) Then, as the saving grace, we added tortillas and hummus. Hippie Bob had an old-fashioned grinder attached to a piece of wood that served as the counter, preparation space, and table. I was assigned to the hummus. My team of three, including myself, got to work funneling garbanzo beans into the grinder. The conversation was quick and light with the usual traveler gab.

As the mound of light-brown mush expanded, the sounds from below grew louder. Someone had discovered an old sweat lodge and a fire was lit for a party sweat. People were preparing early for the event and had started stripping down, eager to enter. Our instructions were to have the meal ready after the completion of the communal sweat. Working away maniacally, adding some spices here, others there, the dinner was looking good. There was just one problem: the hummus. It was so dry and tasteless, that even I didn't want to keep on trying it. I tried to pass it off to someone else, but with no such luck. My teammates had deserted me long ago for the greener pastures of naked bodies stuck together in one small room sweating together, so it was up to me.

What could I add to this? There was nothing except pasta. I considered it for a moment, then struck it off my list and at last in a burst of brilliant inspiration thought: water. Water is good. From childhood we are told to drink eight glasses a day. Water helps your skin, hair, and health, so I figured it could help my hummus. Now remember—we were in Central America where water isn't always the friend you know. There are two types of water: 1. Your best friend—Mr. Agua Pura (pure water). 2. Your worst enemy—Mr. Parasite-Filled Lake Water. Picking up the first jug I saw, I liberally drenched the food. Seconds later, Hippie Bob screamed across the way, "You didn't use the red jug did you, because that is the PARASITE-FILLED LAKE WATER!" Of course I did—what was he thinking, that I knew what I was doing? Everybody stared, shocked, the main staple of our dinner was now ruined and the animal-like sounds of hunger from below were growing more ominous.

"What should we do?" was the general worried question.

"Cook it!" came back the wise reply from the oldest and most experienced travelers in the group. So we did as told, and the hummus bubbled away merrily on the fire for about half an hour until the screams crying for food were unbearable. Dinner was served. As we approached the fire, varying travelers in a state of dress and undress were forming a large semicircle around the glowing embers. All types of plates were brought out, from plastic ones that had seen their prime—to plastic bags and scooped out avocado peels.

Before eating, though, one last Rainbow tradition had to be performed—the meditation and thanks. We all held hands and against the background noise of drums, a flute, and a

Tibetan meditation bowl, we started singing chants of thanks. Usually I don't believe in this crap, but I must say even I was moved by the beauty of the occasion. With a last "*buen provecho*," servers started walking around dishing out generous portions of the hummus, pasta, and tortillas. I didn't want to take the hummus, but then I decided if everybody went down I would too. Gingerly, I spooned the first bite into my mouth—and God it was good! From the murmurs I could tell other people were in agreement. Relaxing and flushed with my success, I began to truly enjoy the evening. I even tried playing the drums and made new friends. When I closed my eyes hours later enclosed in a fluffy sleeping bag, surrounded by unwashed hair including my own, my last thoughts were that I had done well.

Hours later the first groans of pain were heard from the floor somewhere near me. Soon the groans got louder and were joined by others as people made their way outside to join the ranks squatting in the bushes. Instead of people dancing in the dawn, they were crouching on the lawn. My rhyming stopped as the pains began to seize me, and I soon became one of the many. It turns out that everyone in the gathering had gotten the travelers fun and feared friend—*Giardia*!

I had poisoned the peace-loving group. With daybreak the softer traveler's snuck out for the easier comforts of flush toilets (myself included). As the tepee receded in the distance, I watched from a fetal position in the boat and made myself three promises: 1. I would always use bottled water for everything, including brushing my teeth; 2. I would never eat off the street again; 3. I would never cook for anyone I didn't want to poison.

These resolutions reached, I smiled, looking forward to my next gathering and the story this would make for my grandchildren. I never did follow any of those promises, though, and I try to poison people on a daily basis with my cooking, especially my immediate family.

*Armed with her savings and a backpack, Cara Tabachnick spent two years traveling around the world and returned safe, sound, and a whole lot wiser. Born and raised on Long Island, New York (although she doesn't like to admit it), Cara currently lives in New York City where she concentrates on writing, art, helping other people, and just being a better person, which is the best lesson traveling can teach.*

CLEO PASKAL

# The Elephant That Roared

*Like people, countries have personalities.*

THE TOASTMASTER HAS JUST ANNOUNCED THE GAME FOR the evening. Gathered in front of him are over a hundred academics, politicians, intellectual sightseers, and journalists. What we all have in common is an interest—for some an obsession—with the world's smallest countries. We are here, in the Faroe Islands, eighteen tiny specks of incipient nationhood in the North Atlantic, for a conference on the future of microstates (countries with a population of under a million or so).

The game suits us perfectly. The premise: a worldwide competition has been proclaimed for essays about elephants. We have to guess the titles submitted by each country.

The toastmaster starts off the feast of national stereotyping with: "The Americans sent in: 'How to build a bigger and better elephant.' The Japanese countered with: 'How to build a smaller and cheaper elephant.' The English? They proffered: 'Elephants I have shot,' while the French put forward: '*L'amour de l'elephant*.' And the Germans? The Germans sent in seventeen enormous volumes entitled: "A Short Introduction to Elephants.'"

Delegates from some of the larger countries wade in. The professor from northern Russia submits: "Russia, motherland of all elephants." The ever-polite Swedes propose: "How to address an elephant by its proper title." An academic from Northern Ireland throws in: "An essay on why it is not appropriate at this time to decommission our elephants." The self-obsessed Norwegians deign to offer: "Norway and the Norwegians."

We have it now. We know the rules, our challenge is to appropriate this game for microstates. To show that they too have enough of an identity to bother parodying.

A member of the Falkland Islands legislature gets up. There is a hush. Realizing that he will have to acquaint us with the Falklands' sense of self before he can make fun of it, he starts in: "Seeing that the Falkland Islands are stuck out in the middle of the ocean, our essay would be: 'Long-distance swimming techniques for elephants.'" There is a roar of approving laughter, if not for the joke then for the attempt. Maybe we can do this.

Emboldened, by alcohol if by nothing else, an economist from the UK tax haven of Isle of Man tries: "The Isle of Man submits: 'Tax planning for the expatriate elephant.'" The room rocks with laughter. Mixed with relief. We *shall* overcome!

A professor from rabidly free market Estonia booms out: "How to sell an elephant on the New York Stock market." We've got it!

A journalist from the Åland Islands, a group of Swedish-speaking, semiautonomous islands which grudgingly belong to Finland, makes reference to the country's main industry, shipping, with: "How to arrange the transportation of elephants in open seas."

But he's not finished, now it is not enough to create your own national myth, there is growing desire to take shots at the colonial powers. So, a reference to the insecurity of the Finns is included: "And the Finns, they send in: 'An interesting conference on elephants to be held in the lovely town of Helsinki.'"

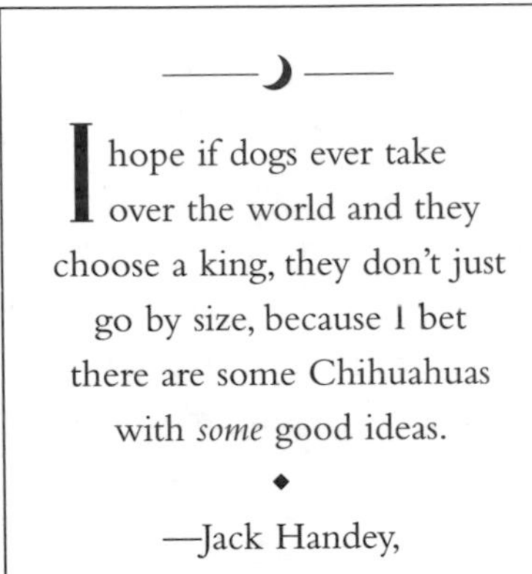

I hope if dogs ever take over the world and they choose a king, they don't just go by size, because I bet there are some Chihuahuas with *some* good ideas.

—Jack Handey, *Deep Thoughts*

About this time, a taciturn economist from the UK decides the atmosphere of self-determination is making us a bit too giddy. He cold showers us with: "The UK's submission is: 'Granting sovereignty to the legs of the elephant so they can each go their own way.'"

We laugh him off good-naturedly. Our microstates are gleaming so brightly tonight, they can eclipse a grumbling number-cruncher with ease.

In fact, even places that are well-ensconced in larger countries are getting a bit heady. A delegate from the University of Prince Edward Island puts forth: "The elephant, is it a federal or provincial responsibility?"

Which prompts the Cape Breton delegate to abduct the whole premise and transform it into not an essay, but a story about his uncle. The uncle had been forced to leave Cape Breton to find work. He managed to get a job with a circus where he found himself assigned to circumcising the elephants. The wages were small but the tips were big.

Things have gone terribly wrong.

Or perhaps not. Representatives are getting so comfortable with their sense of self, they don't feel at all apologetic about having one. We now know to make fun of Ålanders for their shipping, Falkland Islanders for their isolation, and Cape Bretoners for their genial rambling. We have had a peek at each other's soft spots. A sort of cultural group therapy.

Sure, we only know each other through stereotypes, but at least we are starting to know each other, thereby validating the existence of an identity worth making fun of. And, at least in humor, the world's microstates can get laughs as big as the megastates.

In this crowd anyway.

*Cleo Paskal has contributed to many publications including* The Economist *and the* Weekly World News. *She has also hosted two BBC radio travel shows, been a regular TV and radio panelist, taught at universities in the UK, Canada, and New Zealand, and wrote the Emmy-winning TV series "Cirque du Soleil: Fire Within." Her obsession with the world's smallest countries reached its inevitable conclusion when, while in the Republic of the Maldives, a man from the Faroe Islands proposed marriage. And she accepted.*

*

"We Egyptians have funny ideas about America. I myself used to run fruit store in L.A., so I know how it is, but most people in Cairo they think money is everywhere in America. There was one Egyptian man who comes to L.A. His plane lands at LAX and outside on sidewalk he sees a wallet. He can see there is money sticking out from it, but he does not even bend down to pick it up. You know why? He says it is only his first day, and he is not yet ready to start working!"

—Mohammed Kamel, quoted in *Take Me With You,* by Brad Newsham

TIM CAHILL

* * *

# Speaking in Tongues

*While infiltrating a fundamentalist Christian cult in California, the author learns a new skill.*

"YOU MANY THINK YOU CAME HERE FOR A FREE MEAL," THE leader said, "but God drew you here for a very special purpose." He hit briefly on the soul rockers: hellfire, the end of the world, judgment before the Lord, and the Prophecy of the Second Coming before revealing to sinners in the crowd that the biblical promise of eternal life was within our grasps that very evening. All we had to do, it turned out, was to humble ourselves before God—and, of course, everyone else at the service—by kneeling in the little area between the first folding chairs and the pulpit. There we would publicly confess that we led sinful lives in the manner of American POWs taping war crimes confessions before international cameras.

"I put before you this day both a blessing and a curse," he said.

The organist began a churchy solo, and elect Christians threaded through the crowd, looking for obvious sinners. Another short, rather pleasant-looking man in his mid-twenties stood by my chair.

"Why don't you come up and get saved," he stage-whispered.

I shrugged stupidly.

"It's easy," he said. "I'll come with you."

A few sinners and their Christians were moving toward the saving block. The organ finished, stopped momentarily, but at a signal from the man at my side, it started again. The same song. From the top.

"I couldn't say that prayer and mean it," I pointed out.

"It doesn't matter. If you kneel and say it with your lips God will come into your heart in a very special way. Why do you think God brought you here?"

It was difficult to argue the point with every person in the place watching us, so I let myself be led forward to kneel on the hard linoleum floor, under a long fluorescent light. I said the prayer word for word and at no time did I feel God come into my heart, which, I suppose, is as it should be.

"Ahhhhhhhhhhhhhhhhmen," everyone shouted.

A brief announcement before dinner. Baby Christians—the newly saved—had another gift in store for them, "the baptism of the Holy Spirit." Our older Christians would tell us about it.

"God promised that the saved would speak in tongues," I was told by the man who was to become my teacher. "Don't be denied. Seek for the gift with all your heart. Just keep saying, 'God, you promised.'" The process, as it was explained to me, was that one started by "just praising and thanking Jesus." At a certain point, he will begin to stutter, a signal that he is about to begin speaking in tongues. My older Christian invited me into the prayer room to give it a whirl, and since it seemed to be the thing to do after being saved, I followed him through the wooden door.

The room was a windowless expanded closet, perhaps four

steps wide and ten long. There was a muted light in one corner, and as my eyes became accustomed to the darkness, I saw that there were wooden bench seats along three walls and an ancient, puffy sofa along the fourth. The linoleum had been torn up to reveal a wooden floor. The walls were rough-hewn wood, like a rustic sauna.

After the first few seconds of ripping claustrophobia, one became aware of a milling crowd and the monotonic sound of spoken gibberish. People were tromping back and forth lengthwise, and their footsteps produced a constant low rumble, a counterpoint to the words "thank you Jesus, praise you Jesus." Christians stood in various corners and trilled out nonsense syllables: "Ah na na na" and the like at a rapid rate. Talking in tongues.

I was later to happen upon a few verses in Chapter Two of Acts concerning this phenomenon. Forty days after the death of Christ, the Apostles gathered, "And they were all filled with the Holy Ghost, and began to speak with other tongues, as the Spirit gave them utterance." Bystanders were amazed that the Apostles were speaking in their own languages, while, "Others mocking said, 'These men are full of new wine.'"

My older Christian sat me on the bench and took up a position on my right. Someone else sat close by on my left. Both men began rocking back and forth, chanting, "Praise to you Jesus, thank you Jesus."

I have been at Catholic services, where everyone suddenly kneels at some signal, and willy-nilly, I found myself on my knees. It was impossible to remain seated. In the same way, it was difficult to sit in the room and not rock and chant.

"Thank you Jesus, praise you Jesus," I said for a little over an hour.

Presently the three of us began rocking faster, chanting

locomotive-style, "Thank you Jesus, thank you Jesus, thank you Jesus...." I assumed—half-believed—that there was some sort of self-hypnotic process in the works and I intended to get thoroughly stoned. Several people seemed to be in a state of trance. I thought there might be some psychophysiological process in which the tongue spewed out syllables of its own volition after a long chant. For me this was not the case.

"Thank you Jesus," my older Christian said, then began stuttering slightly. "Thank you Jesisisis, thank you jisisisis, dank eh jsiis, dada a jisisisis." I found myself stuttering along. The pace increased and the man on my left broke into tongues. "Ah yab dadaba doedoedoe," he stated. "Ah ra da da da da," the man to my right replied. "Thank ooo jeejecjee," I ventured. Apparently it wasn't enough, and we started the whole process again.

I could not, try as I might, get from the stutter to the tongues organically. I sneaked a look at my watch and realized that I had been rocking and chanting for almost two and a half hours. I was developing an unpleasant prayer sore at the base of my spine, and it was becoming painfully obvious that I wasn't going to get out of there until I began speaking in tongues.

We were working toward another crescendo. "Dank oo jejeje," I said and burst into a tense, conservative burst of tongues. "Er rit ta tit a tit a rit," I said, taking care to roll my *r*'s. "Ah yab a daba daba daba raba," the man on my right shouted. "A nanananan nana nah," the other Christian said.

I opened my eyes slightly on the down rock, saw feet gathering around me and experienced a mainline shot of mortal dread. They knew I wasn't speaking in tongues. They were going to stomp on me like a rat caught in the cheese box. "Er rit a tit tit tita," I babbled, heavy on the rolling *r*'s. "Rit ti tit tit."

There were more feet. Several people stopped chanting and were standing in a semicircle, speaking in loud and extravagant tongues. Someone shouted, "Oh, thank you Jesus, thank you for the victory." The victory, I realized with relief that approached joy, was that I had said, "Rit ti tit tit." I was in. I belonged. Everyone was with me. "Rit ta tit itt, diddla dit dit," I said, introducing a pleasing variant on my basic tongues. This was well received. "Rit a little did a dit diddle dit dit."

Beside me, my older Christian ran through a few change-ups, interspersing his standard "Yab ba da ba da ba" with nice syllables that sounded like the names of biblical towns. "Ah Shal-la-dah, ah shal-ah-dah-dah."

I began to realize that whatever nonsense syllables you said were all right as long as you said them rapidly, in a loud trancelike monotone. It was the best if your tongue bounced rapidly off the roof of your mouth. I tried to come up with some good Old Testament sounds, but the only nonsense that came to mind belonged in old rock and roll songs.

"Ah Sha nana nana nana nana nah," worked excellently. I was confident enough to vary my rhythms. My tongue was very loose. My friends and I took short, increasingly more rapid solos: dueling tongues.

After about twenty minutes, we tapered back down to a half an hour of "praise you Jesus, thank you Jesus." It was past midnight when we left the rat box, and the man who accompanied me to the saving block marked down three and a half hours on a sheet of paper on the outside of the door.

We stood outside the door and finally introduced ourselves. My Christian's name was Frank, and he wanted to know if I would like to stay and serve the Lord. The bus was about to leave.

"Any guests want to go back to Los Angeles?" the driver called.

Frank gave me to believe that my rebirth might not take if I returned to "the World" with its manifold temptations. He said I could backslide into "filth," which he defined as dope, pornography, and possible homosexuality. Women, he said, were often agents of the Devil. I told him I would stay a few days because I was curious about what was involved in "serving the Lord."

Frank shook my hand, said "praise the Lord" and introduced me to several other Christians who greeted my decision with "praise the Lord," uttered in the same vague tone other people say "far out."...

The folding chairs in the church section had been taken up, and the two of us found a spot to sleep right there on the holy linoleum. We formed a small part of a wall-to-wall human carpet consisting of perhaps as many as 125 sleeping men.

"When we get up," Frank said, "we wake up just praising and thanking Jesus." I agreed to wake up praising and thanking and said good night.

"Amen," Frank yawned....

I dropped into a fitful sleep, full of nightmarish disasters, and started awake shortly thereafter overwhelmed with the conviction that something weird was going on. Frank was sitting near my head, a human alarm clock, demonstrating the proper way to wake up when you've just been saved.

"Praise you Jesus thank you Jesus praise you Jesus thank you Jesus praise you Jesus thank you Jesus praise you Jesus thank you Jesus praise you Jesus thank you Jesus...."

My Thank you Jesuses were as cold and hard and artificial as the linoleum floor I had slept on.

"The Lord loves a broken spirit," Frank told me. My soul, apparently, was in danger, and the signs could be read in the sleepy sullenness on my face. We had rolled up our gear and were stepping over some still-sleeping bodies, moving into the bathroom, which was pervaded with an unpleasant diarrhealike odor. The two sit-down toilets were in constant use, and I made an immediate vow of voluntary constipation for the duration of my stay. Showers were out of the question because the stall was already half full of blankets and sleeping bags. A speaker above the last sink spewed out scratchy Bible verses: Leviticus it was, information on how to offer sacrifices, what to do when the smoke doesn't rise, how to tell the difference between what is holy and unholy, what is clean and what is unclean.

"Hallelujah," the brothers said, standing before the filthy sinks. There was no hot water and my sink filled to the top and overflowed because the drain didn't work. It had to be emptied with a cup into a floor waste pipe. It occurred to me that it was best to keep the mind firmly focused on Jesus in a crowded stink-hole like this: Satan was ever-present, trying to pump the brothers full of pride....

Later, we stopped into the prayer room for a quick half-hour chant, then spent a few excruciating hours while Frank read aloud, stumbling over the big words in Matthew, chapters one through six. I felt surly and argumentative. We came onto a verse in which Jesus instructs the multitudes not to pray using "vain repetitions, as the heathens do...."

"Wait a minute," I said, "we just spent half an hour saying 'praise Jesus' in there."

Frank considered the problem in a sincere, furrow-browed

silence. Three older brothers were summoned for a booth-side conference, out of my range of hearing. After several minutes, one of the strange brothers approached with the answer.

"The repetitions," he said severely, "are not vain."

"Of course." I slapped my forehead, Dumbo-style. "I should have known."

"After you've been here for a while and are older in the Lord, you'll be able to think better."

"Thank you Jesus."

"Praise the Lord."

"Hallelujah."

"Thank you Jesus."

"Praise the Lord."

*Tim Cahill is a contributing editor for* National Geographic Adventure *and the author of many books including* A Wolverine Is Eating My Leg, *from which this story was excerpted. He lives in Montana, and shares his life with Linnea Larson, two dogs, and two cats.*

*

Evaluating what everyone was wearing—or not wearing—I quickly discerned that Southern Baptists have little influence here. That's not to say the festivities don't have religious roots, for the whole purpose of Mardi Gras is to give up lint for forty days. Everyone—women especially—are incessantly lifting their blouses to be checked: no lint brings great cheers from the crowd. Since the competition is stiff, many wear outfits that readily assure themselves attention. Yet many people, men and women, fearing the embarrassment of having lint found on their bodies, wear masks. And while on the subject of religion, I never—until New Orleans—had seen a nun in a see-through habit before.

—Whit Deschner, *Travels with a Kayak*

"I can't believe you missed the Canaan exit! ...
The next one isn't for 40 years!"

By permission of Leigh Rubin and Creators Syndicate.

BRAD NEWSHAM

# Show Me the Money

*Some stories you really don't want to hear.*

IT'S 2:30 A.M. ON A QUIET TUESDAY NIGHT/WEDNESDAY morning, and I'm cruising San Francisco's Mission District looking for one last fare. I'm stopped for a red light at Twenty-third and Guerrero—no cars moving for the seven or eight blocks I can see in front of me, none moving in the rear-view, no pedestrians on the street anywhere. The city's gone to sleep.

And then I see him. A man standing in the middle of the road, about a block straight ahead of me, waving one arm. I blink my headlights. He stops waving, but he doesn't move from the middle of the street.

I flick my automatic door locks down, and when the light goes green I drive toward him. But my antennae stay on alert—anything out of the ordinary, especially in the dead of night in this not-the-greatest part of town, makes a cabdriver wary. And the fact that this guy has yet to move out of the middle of the road is certainly out of the ordinary.

I stop the cab several feet in front of him. He looks O.K.

in my headlights—clean-shaven Latino, about twenty-five years old, short dark hair, white sport shirt. He strolls around to my passenger-side window. I push my control button and roll it halfway down.

"Where are you going?" I ask, finger on the door lock, foot poised on the accelerator.

He gives an address in Bernal Heights. I can picture the block—it's on a well-kept street in a well-kept neighborhood. But there's something amiss in his facial expression—he seems stunned. "Are you all right?"

"I was robbed," he says.

Every cabdriver has met drunk "robbery victims" looking for a free ride home. "Are you hurt?" I ask.

"No," he says. "I'm all right."

"Do you have any money?"

Perhaps he misunderstands me. He throws one arm up in the air—awkwardly. He sighs, like I've needlessly accused him of something. "I ain't got no *weapon*!" he cries.

Clearly he's not all there. But judgments are quick on the street, and something tells me he's harmless. I flip up the door locks and watch across the seat back as he opens the rear door. And now I notice something I don't ever remember noticing about a passenger before. This guy's pants are on *inside out*, with the big white pockets sticking out like elephant ears. Also, these inside-out pants are riding very, very low. My passenger is holding them up with one hand—that's why his one-arm-flinging gesture looked so strange. And I don't suppose there's a person in the world who wouldn't have noticed this detail: his entire pubic region is exposed. Plus an inch or two of limp penis. "Well," I think, "at least it's not...*agitated*." As he slumps down onto my back seat I catch a whiff of alcohol.

I've seen plenty of him already, but before we get started, there's one more thing. "I'm going to have to see your money," I tell him.

"O.K., sure," he says. "I got money." He starts grabbing at his right front pocket, and outlined inside the cloth I can see something that sure looks like a wad of bills. But, the pants being on inside out, the guy is having all sorts of trouble getting at them. (To help visualize, you might try this at home right now—just turn your own pocket inside out and imagine a wad of bills inexplicably "inside.")

So while he's writhing around, trying to figure how to get into his own pants, I glide slowly around the corner and come to a stop in front of the police station at Twenty-third and Valencia. I slip the cab into park and turn around to give the guy my full attention. He looks up from his back seat yoga session and notices all the police cruisers parked in front of the station. I see it register on his face—not as fright, just as one more indignity to deal with. He starts digging harder at his pants, but he still can't get at whatever's inside.

"Look," I say, "why don't you stick your hand *inside* your pants?" It occurs to me that I've never uttered those words to a passenger before—or to anyone. "You might reach it that way."

"I got money," he says, and now he grabs the whole inside-out pocket that he can't get his hand into, and starts to yank it right off the trousers. I hear stitches ripping loose.

"Hey!" I say. "Are you sure you want to do *that*?"

"It's O.K...," he says, yanking ever harder at the pocket, grimacing now, and I can hear more stitches shredding. Before the pocket gives up and comes off in his hand with a loud tearing sound; before he digs a ten-dollar bill out of the mutilated cloth and hands it to me; and before I drive him home, a huge smile on my face the whole way—he says something I've never heard from a passenger before, or from anybody—something I did not ask him to explain. Some stories you really don't want to hear.

He's still torturing his pocket, still grimacing, so the words come out strained, one at a time. "It's O.K.," he says. "These...are...not...my...pants."

*Brad Newsham once roamed the globe with a pen. Now he cares for his daughter, Sarah, by day, and roams the streets of San Francisco by night. If you catch him behind the wheel of Cab #9011 and mention this story, he says he'll give you the ride free—"unless it's over five bucks, in which case we can flip double-or-nothing." He is the author of* All the Right Places *and* Take Me With You: A Round-the-World Journey to Invite a Stranger Home. *In 2001 he founded the non-profit Backpack Nation, whose mission is "To transform the West's two to three million independent travelers into an army of global ambassadors, emissaries of peace, a roving force for good, and thereby help to save our world." Brad is now working on a book about life behind the wheel of a San Francisco taxicab.*

DAVE BARRY

# Welcome to Ireland

*But don't forget your earplugs.*

I RECENTLY SPENT A WEEK IN IRELAND, AND I CAN HONESTLY say that I have never been to any place in the world where it is so easy to partake of the local culture, by which I mean beer. Ireland also contains history, nice people, enormous quantities of scenery, and a rich cultural heritage, including (more on this later) Elvis.

Geographically, Ireland is a medium-size rural island that is slowly but steadily being consumed by sheep. It consists mostly of scenic pastures occasionally interrupted by quaint towns with names such as (these are actual Irish town names) Ardfert, Ballybunion, Coole, Cullybackey, Dingle, Dripsey, Emmoo, Feakle, Fishguard, Gweedore, Inch, Knockaderry, Lack, Leap, Lusk, Maam, Meetullynagarn, Muff, Newmarket on Fergus, Nutt's Corner, Oola, Pontoon, Rear Cross, Ringaskiddy, Screeb, Sneem, Spiddal, Spink, Stradbally, Tang, and Tempo.

These towns are connected by a modern, state-of-the-art system of medieval roads about the width of a standard bar of hotel soap; the result is that motorists drive as fast as possible in hopes of getting to their destinations before they meet anybody coming the other way. The only thing that prevents everybody from going 120 miles per hour is the nationwide system—probably operated by the Ministry of Traffic Safety—of tractors being driven very slowly by old men wearing caps; you encounter these roughly every two miles, rain or shine, day or night. As an additional safety measure, the roads are also frequented by herds of cows, strolling along and mooing appreciatively at the countryside, reminding you very much of tour groups.

A typical Irish town consists of several buildings, one of which is always a bar, called a "pub." Next to this there will typically be another pub, which is adjacent to several more pubs. Your larger towns may also have a place that sells food, but this is not critical.

Inside the pubs you will usually find Irish people, who are very friendly to strangers, especially compared with the British, who as a rule will not voluntarily speak to you until you have lived in Britain for a minimum of 850 years. The Irish, on the other hand, will quickly start a conversation with you, and cheerfully carry it on at great length, with or without your help. One evening in a busy Dublin pub I watched an elderly, well-dressed, cap-wearing gentleman as he sat in the corner and, for two solid hours, struck up a lively conversation with every single person or group who sat within ten yards of him, including a group of German tourists, only one of whom spoke even a little English. The man spoke to them in a thick brogue on a variety of topics for several minutes while they looked at him with the bright, polite smiles of people who do not have a clue what is being said to them. When he finished, they conferred briefly in German, and then the one who spoke a little English said, quote, "Everyone is pleased that he or she is welcome."

You definitely feel welcome in Ireland. But there's more to do there than just talk to Irish people in pubs. You can also drive around the countryside, alternately remarking "Look! Sheep!" and "Here's another tractor!" You can visit a bunch of old castles built by the Normans, who at one point conquered Ireland despite being called the "Normans," which is, let's face it, not an impressive-sounding name. It's kind of like being conquered by the "Freds."

Probably the best-known castle is the one in the town of Blarney, which contains the famous Blarney Stone. To get to it, you have to climb steep, narrow, tourist-infested steps to the top of the castle; there, a local man holds you as you lean out over the castle wall and kiss the Blarney Stone. Legend has it that if you do this, you will give the man a tip.

Also at the castle in a town called Kilkenny I saw a local radio station doing a live remote broadcast, featuring a Frozen Food Challenge in which a local resident had to answer a multiple-choice question on the history of refrigeration. She got it right, and won a hamper of frozen foods.

*"Brilliant!"* she said.

But in my opinion the cultural highlight of the trip occurred in the town of Ennis, where a pub called Brandon's had a sign outside that said "Traditional Irish Music." This turned out to be a traditional Irish Elvis impersonator. I realize that there are literally thousands of quality Elvis impersonators, and I'm sure you've seen some excellent ones, but I am here to tell you that this one, in this unremarkable town in western Ireland, was beyond question the worst Elvis impersonator in world history. He sang along to a tape of instrumental Elvis tunes, which he played on a sound system that he never, not once in two solid hours, got adjusted right.

Every time he'd start singing a song, the sound system would screech and honk with feedback; Elvis would then whirl around and spend minutes at a time unsuccessfully adjusting various knobs while he mumbled lyrics, so that for most of the evening all you saw was Elvis's butt, accompanied by screeching and honking and vague off-key singing.

Often, by the time he'd finished twiddling the knobs, Elvis had lost track of what song he was singing; he'd frown into the distance, trying various tunes until he thought he was on the right track, at which point inevitably the screeching and honking would start up, forcing Elvis to whirl back around, like a man being attacked by bees, and treat the audience to another lengthy view of his butt.

The crowd, which I will frankly admit was consuming alcoholic beverages, enjoyed this performance immensely, cheering wildly at the end of each song. They like their fun, the Irish. I'm definitely going back some day. Maybe I'll rent a tractor.

*Dave Barry is a Pulitzer Prize-winning syndicated columnist at the* Miami Herald. *His books include* Homes and Other Black Holes, Dave Barry's Greatest Hits, Dave Barry Slept Here, *and* Dave Barry Turns 40, *among others. He plays lead guitar in a literary rock band called the Rock Bottom Remainders, whose other members include Stephen King, Amy Tan, Ridley Pearson, and Mitch Albom. They are not musically skilled, but they are extremely loud. In his spare time, Dave is a candidate for president of the United States. If elected, his highest priority will be to seek the death penalty for whoever is responsible for making Americans install low-flow toilets.*

DOUG LANSKY

* * *

# Bad Haircuts Around the World

*It's not easy to get a little trim.*

I HAVE NO IDEA WHAT ADVENTURE TRAVEL IS ANYMORE. These days, nearly any activity—including getting momentarily disoriented at a cruise ship buffet table—counts as adventure travel. But if you want to push the envelope by the seat of your pants on the edge of the wild side, then I suggest you take a crack at a serious travel adventure: namely, getting a haircut in a developing nation for less than $3 from someone you can only communicate with via hand signals, except that your hands are covered by the barber's smock.

I've had the spiritual bowl cut while sitting on the ghat steps in Varanasi, India, and a spastically uneven chop from a fourteen-year-old in Hanoi. And I thought I had a pretty decent clip from a semiblind man with a chair on the sidewalk in Beijing, though when he set up the double mirror so I could see the back of my head, I noticed he had brought my hairline up about even with the tops of my ears. When viewed from the rear, travelers pointed out, it looked as if my neck was about nine inches long and extended up to the top of my head.

The point is, I never quite know what I'm in for when I get my hair cut on the road—sometimes literally on the road, sitting on the curb holding a cracked mirror fragment with a guy chopping away behind me with a pair of scissors that wouldn't make a straight cut through a Post-it note. But I've found that most of these barbers subscribe to the hair-cutting theory that the more they take off, the better deal they're giving you for your money, and the happier you'll be. So they never quite know when to stop.

This chop-till-you-drop style was most noticeable in a sixty-something Brazilian barber I nicknamed Edward Scissor-hands, who clipped my hair with the aid of what appeared to be Parkinson's disease. I should have taken more notice of his enthusiasm for cutting, as he was snipping away at the air when I walked into his parlor. I had a ponytail when I sat down for a trim, and by the time I got out of his chair, I looked like an intern for the Christian Coalition. I had to actually jump out of the chair and physically restrain Edward from going Kojak on me.

Now that my hair is relatively short, I face another problem with barbers: the trim. I always make the same mistake of indicating the amount of trim I desire by showing the barber roughly a quarter inch of space between my thumb and index finger. I am trying to convey that the quarter inch is the amount I wish to have taken off. Invariably, the barbers interpret this quarter inch as the amount of hair I wish to remain on my head. And after about thirty seconds of free-hand snipping, that's all I have left on one side of my scalp. I see the damage when they present me with the mirror, and I am reluctantly forced to concede the same style on the other side of my head.

But the most interesting part of the haircut often has nothing to do with the haircut. In Turkey, they don't stop with the hair on the top of your head. Apparently, any hair located above the chest is fair game. Before I knew what was happening, I had my eyebrows trimmed and my nostrils dehaired while the barber's assistant rolled two pieces of thread back and forth on my upper cheekbone then yanked them, removing an entire area of blond micro hairs I didn't even know I had (although after this procedure, my hair grew back darker and more pronounced, and I'm now forced to shave higher on my cheek—practically right up to my eyeball). One Turkish barber even tried to shave my forehead. I grabbed his wrist and put a quick stop to that plan. I may not have any visible hair on my forehead now, but I probably would if I had let him shave it. It was no small feat to leave Turkey after forty-five days without looking like an extra in *Planet of the Apes*.

The best part of the Turkish haircut is the neck crack you get at the end. Most barbers have perfected this chiropractic art. The first time, however, it comes as a bit of a shock; it really feels like they're ripping your head off. They generally just twist until something snaps, and if you're lucky, it's not your spinal cord.

In Vietnam one barber volunteered to clean my ears. Why not? Using a head-mounted camping flashlight and—I'm pretty sure about this—shish kebab skewers, he began excavating the wax from inside my ear. The scraping sounded like an amplified version of what the dentist does on your teeth with his metal pick. Unsettling, but not painful. From my ear, he then produced a ball of wax that would have been sufficient to coat a surfboard.

Using a finer probe, he dug even further, sending me into a fit of coughing. As I began hacking, my instinct was to grab his hand and steady the sharp probe. But before I could make contact, he pulled back swiftly, taking with him some remaining refuse from my inner sanctum—and possibly a small portion of my brain—in the process.

Then he began flicking me behind the ear with his finger in what I imagine was an effort to loosen any remaining wax. To sweep up the debris, he inserted a miniature feather duster, or maybe a paint brush, and began twirling it around. This had the audio effect of a wasp stuck in my eardrum, and in all likelihood it coated my ear with the wax debris from the person he used it on last. At least I had the comfort of knowing that my earwax debris would be transferred to the next adventure traveler, thus contributing my small part to this rich tradition.

*Doug Lansky is the author of* Last Trout in Venice, Up the Amazon Without a Paddle, First Time Around the World, *and the syndicated newspaper feature "Signspotting." He is also editor of* There's No Toilet Paper on the Road Less Traveled, *which won the Independent Publisher's Book Award. He is a popular speaker on world travel and lives in Sweden with his wife and three daughters.*

*

The third beautician in the Bangkok parlor arrived with Miss Pat our translator, who told us the ladies wanted to ask an important question. "Shoot away," I said. I would have agreed to anything.

"What you mean, shoot?"

"I mean, ask the question."

"These ladies are hearing your voice, and they are thinking about a friend living in your country. You are talking like their friend. Maybe, they think, you are knowing him?"

"What's his name?" I wondered, considering more than 200 million possibilities.

"His name John Wayne. You are knowing John Wayne?"

I lied and did not mention his death. "Of course, I know him. The Duke."

"Ahhhh," they chorused. "The Duck."

"The Duck," I said.

"Duck," Miss Pat repeated. "They are happy you are knowing the Duck."

They charged me thirty baht, a dollar and a half, for a haircut and massage. What kind of a discount, I wondered, had they given me for knowing the Duck?

—Burley Packwood, *Bird Turd Peppers and Other Delights*

ADAIR LARA

# Fear of Not Flying

*When do we board?*

BILL AND I WERE LEAVING SAN FRANCISCO FOR A FLIGHT TO New York. I was nervous, as usual, about missing the plane, and he was nervous, as usual, about getting to the airport too early. (He's what the airlines call a "runner"—one of those people who like to run to the gate at the last minute to catch their flight.)

He's so scared of getting there early that he asked me to call Supershuttle and tell them our flight was at ten, instead of its actual time, nine, so we could cut it as close as possible.

As everybody knows, I am a compliant wife, so I called the shuttle and lied, as he asked. Only I said our flight left at eight.

Well, I'm sorry, but I worry. I'd like to be a "runner," dashing through the airport at the last minute, with twelve outfits cunningly packed into an overnight bag, then sweep through the gate in a cloud of Chanel No. 5, tossing a boarding pass over my shoulder to the attendant.

But it's not me. If I were that late I'd be sweating and worrying, with my purse slipping down my arm and my bags banging against my ankles, looking as if I'd been chased into the airport by a hostile mob.

Bill was still in the shower when the shuttle driver rang the doorbell. I was ready, two suitcases and a garment bag waiting by the door. We were going for only a week, but when I travel, I like to be prepared for a freak snowstorm, a power outage, an invitation to the White House, anything. Bill, of course, had everything in one carry-on garment bag, ready for the last-minute swan dive into the 747 as it pulled away from the gate.

"What?" he said when I pounded on the door and said the shuttle was here.

"The clock must be slow," I said brightly. "Anyway, they're here, so could you hurry up?"

As we sped toward the airport, I kept an eye on the shuttle driver to make sure he made no more than the three stops he's allowed. I was sure this would be the day a truck of leghorn chickens would overturn on the freeway.

Bill, his hair still damp, gaped at his watch in disbelief when we arrived at SFO. "We have over an hour to wait!" he gasped.

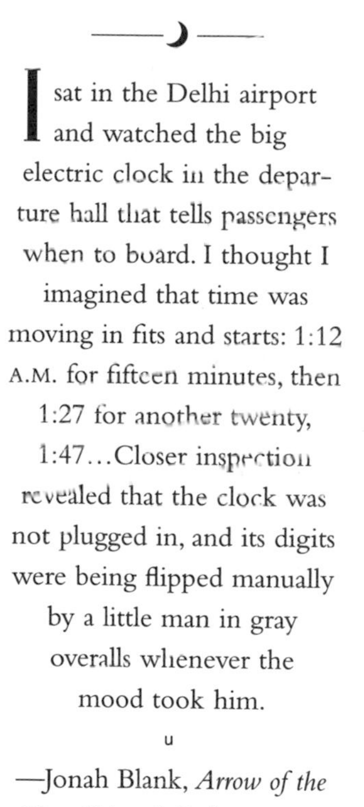

I sat in the Delhi airport and watched the big electric clock in the departure hall that tells passengers when to board. I thought I imagined that time was moving in fits and starts: 1:12 A.M. for fifteen minutes, then 1:27 for another twenty, 1:47...Closer inspection revealed that the clock was not plugged in, and its digits were being flipped manually by a little man in gray overalls whenever the mood took him.

—Jonah Blank, *Arrow of the Blue-Skinned God: Retracing the Ramayana Through India*

"I know," I said worriedly. "It's not that much time. And I still have to check my bags."

When we got to the gate with fifty-five minutes to spare, I relaxed for the first time. I had time to browse the airport shops, have a cup of coffee, and use the rest room near the gate instead of standing in line fighting with two-year-olds over the tiny one on the plane.

"At least we know we won't miss the plane," I said to Bill. Secretly I'm sure that if you don't make your flight they clap a dunce cap on you with a sign saying, "This idiotic couple missed their plane."

"We could have missed our plane and caught the next one in the time we're sitting here." He grumbled, sitting down. I could tell by his face that he was sorry he hadn't suggested we say good-bye to each other in the kitchen and meet at Rockefeller Center, by the ice skating rink.

He paced, he sat, he read. Finally, as they began to board our flight, he announced that he was going to the bathroom.

"You're going to the bathroom now?" I said.

"There's plenty of time," he said. "They never leave on time, and it's stuffy sitting on the plane."

He took the tickets with him. And I waited, his garment bag and my purse slung over my shoulder, while they called the passengers for first class, then the rest of us, row by row. As I heard "Last call for flight 809 to New York," calm descended on me. We were going to get the dunce cap after all.

The last passenger had disappeared into the jet way, and the last airline attendant was wheeling her little suitcase aboard when Bill flew by me. "Come on!" he yelled. And we sprinted for the plane, getting on at the last minute, just as he wanted.

*Adair Lara is the author of* Normal Is Just a Setting on the Dryer *and* Hold Me Close, Let Me Go. *This story was excerpted from her book* The Best of Adair Lara: Award Winning Columns from the San Francisco Chronicle.

*

"Ladies and gentlemen," announced the conductor in our carriage as the train came to a grinding halt, "this train has caught fire. Please exit the train and walk in single file to the first-level crossing where you will be met by a bus. Do not touch the live rail, under any circumstances. I repeat, do not touch the live rail. It's the one in the middle of the track. No, hang on, isn't it the one on the left? I used to know this. Bugger."

People in the carriage slowly started to gather their belongings.

"Just to keep you informed, ladies and gentlemen," added the conductor as I reached for my rucksack, "it appears that the fire is due to an excessive buildup of friction in the undercarriage."

"It wasn't me," said Paul, returning from the toilet.

—Stewart Ferris and Paul Bassett, *Don't Mention the War!: A Shameful European Adventure*

"Sir, the airline insists that luggage must match the passenger."

Cartoon by Benita Epstein

NICHOLAS DELBANCO

* * *

# April Fool

*In which the tables are turned*
*in the south of France.*

WE GAVE A TEA PARTY ON APRIL 1. WE INVITED FOUR COUPLES—all elderly, all Europeans—to the little house. They had entertained us often, turn by turn; it was our chance to reciprocate. We bought patisserie by the box-full, tarts and fruit and cake. They were engineers, and brokers, and retired chemists, grave and kindly citizens, courtly men with stiff-brimmed hats, the women wearing gloves.

What imp of the perverse possessed me I can no longer tell. But it came to me, preparing, that this was April Fool's Day and we should observe it; we could introduce them to the time-honored custom of practical jokes. "A custom better honored in the breach," Elena said, and I said, no, we ought to do it, it would be terrific fun. We would start the meal with joke food and then repair to the real treats that waited covered on the sideboard or in the chill *cave*.

So we did the whole thing wrong—preparing coffee and tea, then spicing it, pouring vinegar in wine and pepper in the chocolate sauce, adding mustard to the jam. All the uproarious tricks of a ten-year-old returned to me—the whoopee cushion, the preshredded napkin, salt in the sugar bowl, dirt on the fork. I could scarcely contain my excitement; it seemed like the most fun in years.

When they arrived, we were waiting. We were mannerly, polite. We showed them the house, the flowers, the grounds; we discussed the weather and politics and how innocent the American people were as to corruption, how we failed to take it for granted, making molehill-mountains out of fraud and greed. They said that we were lucky, marvelously fortunate, and that youth—ourselves excepted, *naturellement*—is wasted on the young.

We sat. We offered wine, cake, and tea. Tittering, I poured while Elena cut and served. They tasted the first mouthful, expressionless, then ate. I had been waiting for the burst of laughter, the telltale recognition, dawning joke, the way we'd grin and explain it away, the proper feast to come.

Instead, and to my horror, they proceeded with the meal. They said how skilled we were, how domestically practiced; they even asked Elena for the recipe. "Where did you learn to cook?" one woman inquired— at whose house we had consumed a splendid six-course supper just the week before. Her question did not sound sarcastic. She drank the undrinkable brew. When her husband asked for seconds, I had had enough. I said the joke was over now, my little game was stupid, they did not need to continue. The cake was inedible, clearly; my own piece lay untouched.

"*Mais non*," they said. "Don't be unkind. It's an excellent *gâteau*."

"*Gâté*," I said. "It's spoiled. We made it this way on purpose. It's April Fool's, you see."

"April Fool's?"

"The first of April. *Un gâteau gâté*—a spoiled cake. On this day we play practical jokes."

"How sweet of you," they said, "to make excuses for your wife. But she doesn't require them, truly. She will learn to bake."

"She knows it already," I said.

"How very sweet."

"How gallant. *Les jeunes mariés*."

"I'll have some more," said the excellent cook, "of your excellent coffee. *Merci*."

I have not played an April Fool's joke since.

*Nicholas Delbanco is a novelist and essayist, the author of several books including* Fathering, In the Middle Distance, *and* Running in Place: Scenes from the South of France, *from which this story was excerpted.*

RICHARD STERLING

* * *

# Mr. Disguise

*Going back to Vietnam for the umpteenth time, he decided to be someone else.*

I ARRIVED IN SAIGON OCTOBER 30TH, A SATURDAY AFTER-noon, seven hours late from Hong Kong. Nobody here has ever seen me with a beard, and most know me with a shaved head, the guy who does the Captain Picard impression. I resolved to fool them all with my newly shifted shape.

Case 1: I donned big sunglasses, pulled my hat down low over my eyes, and slouched into Headquarters (Hien's Bar) like a private dick working a case. Outside the tropical sun blazed and glared with painful brightness. But inside the bar the shadowy gloom wrapped around me like a trench coat. There she was, behind the bar. Gorgeous as usual, dressed in one of those silk *ao dai* she always wears. She still had that pouty look she gets when no one is there to tell her what a doll she is. Yeah, it was her, the divine Miss Hang. When she turned and looked up at me, a lock of her thick, midnight hair fell over one eye, Veronica Lake style. "Ha," I thought. "I've got her blindsided. She'll never recognize me now."

I took a seat at the far end of the bar. Without a word she

turned and walked toward the cooler, and through the split tunic of her garment offered me glimpses of those long, long legs that start at the surface of the Earth and go all the way up to Paradise. She opened the cooler and, as if reaching for a switchblade, grabbed a cold one. Off came the top in one flick of the wrist, the spent cap clattering on the marble floor and worshipping at those platform-shod feet. All as if to say, "I do that to guys like you all the time."

She walked slowly down the length of the bar, pouring the suds into a tall glass as she moved. With a cool hand and a keen eye she lifted the bottle ever higher as she poured and walked, skillfully building up a creamy, frothy head that threatened to overexcite itself and foam over the top to lave her hand in its whiteness. But at the last possible moment she stopped her tease with a skill born of innumerable such non-conclusions. She set the bubbling frustrated drink down in front of me. "Why you get hairy face?" she demanded. "And why you gone so long?"

"What? Huh? You recognize me?"

"And you get new hat, too. I like the other one better."

"But I'm in disguise."

"You don't disguise from me. You think I don't know how you walk? Besides, you got a big head. Anybody can see. You want to play Jenga? I beat you again like always."

"But I'm in disguise."

"Where your friend Garrett?"

"I'm Garrett, dammit! I'm in disguise!"

"You drink your beer, Mr. Disguise. I get the Jenga game. Beat you again."

After losing three straight games, I decided that I looked down enough in the mouth and could walk in a sad enough shuffle to fool someone with my disguise.

Case 2: I went to the Hot Chile Bar. There the Russian-speaking Miss Huyen burst out the door at my approach, threw her little body at mine for one of the Russian bear hugs she learned at school and hollered, "Tovarich! You come back!"

"You recognise me already? But I'm in disguise, *da*?"

"*Nyet.* You very bad spy. Better you drink beer."

I drank beer. Then I went to all the other usual spots. Everywhere my brilliant disguise was of no use. It was as though I hadn't even gone to Spain, grown my hair and beard and bought a new hat. It was as though I had just gone to the men's room and stayed a little longer than usual.

Case 3: Finally, in total defeat, I went to the Rolling Stone Bar. I walked in and told Miss Thuyet to set me up with the usual. "What usual?" she asked.

"The usual usual," I said. She just looked at me quizzically.

"Don't you know me?"

"No," she said, looking closely.

"Bless you."

Her look of intense scrutiny began to soften. A gleam appeared in her eye and a little smile began to curl her lips. She opened a BGI beer, poured it into a mug and set it before me, and winked.

"Welcome back, Richard." Case closed.

*Richard Sterling is a graduate of the University of California, Berkeley, and a veteran of seven years in the U.S. Navy. He is the author of* The Fire Never Dies, How to Eat Around the World, *and several books in Lonely Planet's World Food series. He's also the editor of* The Adventure of Food: True Stories of Eating Everything, *and the award-winning* Travelers' Tales Food: A Taste of the Road. *He lives in Oakland, California.*

*"Are you pretty good with your fists?"*

MICHAEL LANE AND JIM CROTTY

# Close Encounters of the California Kind

*It's hot out there, as two guys called the Mad Monks get stuck in traffic.*

HALF PAST TEN ON A MONDAY MORNING, INCHING DOWN 101 past the Ventura Freeway, the Econoline boiled under the orange haze of the Valley, as eight lanes of traffic inched slowly forward.

Nurse, our cat, sat across the engine hub, draped lifeless in the sweltering smog heat, tongue fully extended and ribs pumping for oxygen.

"He's panting. I think he's going to croak if we don't do something."

"Throw some water on him," Jim advised.

"No, no, no! Don't throw water on him. That's the worst thing to do."

"But he won't drink any of his kitty water."

"Just let him pant. That's the only way he'll cool down."

Nurse continued to wheeze. The weatherman reported record ozone alert, temperature inversion, and no end to the dry, crisp, brown sunny skies that had been plaguing L.A. for weeks.

"Ninety-two degrees in here and we don't have air. Look at all those bimbos with their air-conditioning blaring. That's half the problem...all these cars," Jim Nader complained. "I just can't fucking believe this town. Ten million people and no mass transit. It's absolutely insane!"

"Jim, you should talk. What do you think we're driving?"

"I know—it's a koan I've been trying to resolve since we began this journey. We're part of the problem. We should be walking, not driving." Jim gazed morosely at the white divider bumps on the freeway as they slowly inched by. "This is ridiculous. I could walk to Hollywood faster than you can drive," Jim mumbled angrily.

Just then a lightbulb went off. "Look, talk is cheap. Time for action. Hey, Nurse, wanna take a walk?"

Jim bolted out the door leading Nurse by his leash, weaving slightly ahead of Econoline.

"Jim, Jim, what the hell are you doing!" Mike screamed out the van window.

Cars inched along as Jim the Mad Monk greeted drivers with a wave and a *gassho*, steering Nurse clear of wheels.

"Get the fuck in the van...are you fucking out of your mind?" Mike screeched.

Jim paid no mind.

He was now far ahead, alongside a silver-trimmed white Pontiac, when a young woman rolled down her window, allowing a cool blast of air to hit Jim across the arm.

"Whoa. What was that?" Jim turned.

"Air-conditioning. You and your kitty want a ride?"

Jim's eyes bulged open wide. The Valley girl was *stacked*, cleavage literally tumbled out of her tank top. Her wall of dark hair was pulled out of her face. "Come on, get in! He's not going anywhere in a hurry," she said referring back to Mike.

"Ha ha ha ha ha." Jim laughed at the thought. "I mean really, c'mon, I mean, really, you know I gotta…I mean, this is too much."

"Get in, Destiny's calling!"

Jim pulled on the leash and gathered Nurse in his arms, entering the passenger side with a big smile and a bow to the cars as Mike angrily threw up his hands. At four cars behind there was nothing a responsible Monk could do.

"Just be a second!" Jim smiled toward Mike.

Mike was *fuming.*

Inside purred the metaphysical melodies of Ray Lynch. The woman was talking nonstop on her car phone when the Mad Monk first entered her inner sanctum.

"If we took responsibility for the mother and wed our desires to her desires, our lives would find no resistance. We bleed inside for her wounds. We *are* her wounds."

She winked at Jim as she continued weaving the listener through her goddess babble.

"Hi!" She turned to Jim, hanging up. "Welcome to my ashram."

Inside, the car had the aroma of three, four, maybe five cultures in collision— carpeted like a low-rider cruise ship, shag covering the floor and dash, purple no less, with bucket seats that were upholstered with a Tibetan rug and sandalwood incense that burned out of an ashtray, not to mention two dozen crystals of various sizes hanging off the mirror. In the back sat a laptop computer.

The woman looked over and smiled through her pink-glossed lips and fluorescent-pink shades. "You can call me Ariel. I'm going into my male. I'm queen of the subconscious. And for your education and enjoyment I'm also a little girl, playful clown, wise sage, seductress, high priestess, and modern woman on the run. All right, Romeo, who you be?"

Jim was mesmerized. But for only a moment.

"I'm the Mad Monk."

"What are you so mad about Mr. Monk?"

"I didn't sleep last night!"

"Oh, well, you can throw yourself in my back seat if you want. But no, I want you up here." She gave Jim a pat on the leg and a come-hither look.

Ariel was camped out in a big cushy bucket seat with an amethyst crystal overhead. Now the tape switched to Gregorian chants as rainbow prisms danced across the ceiling.

"Gregorian chant. I like it." Jim settled into his bucket seat, drifting off to grade school basketball fantasyland, enjoying the ozone-depleting conditioned air. Even Nurse drifted off into the Buddha fields, his panting finally coming to a stop.

Ariel was suddenly in a trance of her own...but a very different style of trance. It seemed she was either hurting or rejoicing, as tears streamed down her soft face. Or maybe she was allergic to Nurse. Or just emotionally housecleaning. Jim couldn't tell.

"There is a reason for every moment," she said. "and there's a reason we met on the road just now. There's some way we're all going to grow in this."

*Is she stoned*? Jim was a sensitive creature himself, prone to tears, a "We Are the World" kind of guy, but *wasn't she getting a bit melodramatic*?

"Why are you crying?" he asked tenderly.

"Oh, it must be that damn cat of yours. God knows I just adore those creatures, but I can't get within a foot of them without going crazy. Zoran says I'm allergic because I was Cleopatra in a past life. But I love you. I know there must be something we're going to heal in each other because I've been so lonely and there you were, just walking down the street. You came for me!"

Jim noticed Ariel's pendulous breasts hanging loosely out of her tank top. Not in any philandering sort of way, just noticing the blunt forthrightness of her total approach. *Either this woman is a New Age nymphomaniac or this is God speaking and I am called to be her slave.*

"Do you know we're going into a full-moon cycle? Three days to prepare and then we're there. Nirvana! Just collect the energy, then three days to shake it all out. Seven days of bliss," Ariel said with a sigh.

"You know, this morning I was eating breakfast and every bite was like a metaphor," she continued. "Washing dishes was like a ceremonial baptism at the sink. It was like I was drifting into a timeless zone in which nothing was held back or refused." Ariel took one of those deep breaths they teach you at rebirthing workshops. "I think every feeling should be explored to its roots, don't you?"

"Oh totally."

There was a quiet pause as Ariel gently grabbed for Jim's hand.

"Do you mind if I ask you a personal question?" Jim said.

"Please do. All we have is the personal. I believe the more personal the better. The personal is political."

"Tell me, tell, gosh, this will sound really weird. O.K., O.K.—no, no, I can't."

Jim had this habit of announcing a question, but after checking with Gemini Control, deciding not to ask it.

"Please, please, get personal. What is it you seek to know, Mr. Monk?"

"Are you on Ecstasy?" Jim blurted.

"We should share our ecstatic dreams. Last night I dreamt

about violence and a chase through African villages with the squealing noise of women. Someone's laundry was still hanging on the line. They'd talked so late into the night they forgot to bring it in, two days in a row. It was growing mold on it." Ariel giggled.

"You're on Ecstasy, aren't you?"

"I'm on life. It's a drug without the side effects." She took another one of those deep, meaningful rebirthing breaths.

Traffic inched along as incense wafted through the car creating an aromatic fog. So dense, Jim began to feel as if the car were on something.

"Your car is loaded. Hey, I'm impressed. How do you do this?"

Ariel didn't hear it.

The mood kept changing. It wasn't just her. It was everyone on the freeway together. Somehow, from inside the Pontiac, everyone looked high on Ecstasy.

"What's with your windows? Everyone looks like they're flying!"

"Look at us. We create amazing synergy, and any second things could totally change. Whatever we think now might soon be out of context. Bigger and bigger pictures will keep taking hold." Her voice droned on in a soft purr, caressing the words, as she took those deep deep breaths, staring ahead with a beaming smile as if she were moving straight toward the Light.

"I'm into crystals and gemstones."

Jim was tempted to phone Stanislav Grof to see if this qualified as a "spiritual emergency."

"If you wear rose quartz beads around your neck, your heart will open up."

*Everyone is your teacher. Every situation is your teacher.* Jim was remembering the recent affirmation he'd read and was trying desperately to follow its edict. But the Mad Monk was skeptical.

"I'm just getting into crystals," she said, "and there are so many things to learn with each stone. They are the most ancient and solid form. Rose quartz will break down the resistance to love. I want you to wear these." She handed Jim a necklace of stones the size of golf balls.

"Wear these?"

Within minutes Jim was swearing Ariel was right. There *was* less tension. His resistance *was* broken. He felt his heart muscles pulling him toward her. His groin muscles were working overtime.

Michael was sitting in the van two cars back when he saw them kiss. Michael's head hit the ceiling.

"Can you believe that? What a tramp. He jumps in the car and now they're making out. I don't believe this!"

The Pontiac was filled with fragrance. Jim felt as if he were sinking into the seat as shafts of light swept up the rear window rushing off the ceiling. Vangelis blasted "Chariots of Fire." Jim's stomach tightened with unbearable excitement.

Michael felt as if he'd passed out in the heat. Leaning on his horn was of no use, as every other car was doing the same, sending a cacophony of sound toward the ozone.

Ariel's car phone rang and she halted the kiss, going off into another dimension. And she began talking and talking and talking. Then she began praying. It overcame her. Jim sat stunned.

"My soul hungers for seeds of truth that might bear fruit in times of need," she cried into the phone. Then hung up.

The kissing resumed and the traffic continued to inch forward. Michael could see Jim's hand down her blouse. They were talking.

"Nurse's Aide. Nurse's Aide, what are they saying?" Michael strained to read lips.

"Do you have a job? How 'bout a boyfriend?" Jim was asking.

She didn't hold a job, but she was working. Her work was comforting lost souls. And she was on her way to the Whole Life Expo. Jim wanted to go. But then she began crying.

"What's going on with you, Ariel?" Jim asked.

"I feel like I'm burning up. Something is eating me inside. I feel horrible, like I'm going to die."

"My God, pull over! Are you serious? Maybe it's the incense, it's pretty thick in here. Could that be it?"

Ariel started to talk feverishly about commitment. "We run from commitment. But that's because we often cause our commitment with another person to become a limitation. We paint the brighter picture elsewhere and create fear with what we have so that we will eventually run away."

"Why are you telling me this, Ariel?" Jim felt as if he'd found another mind reader.

"So you can get back to your father and mother."

"My father and mother? What do they have to do with it?"

"I mean mother earth and father sky."

Jim turned to look through the back window and could see the Econoline now five cars behind. Michael was slumped on the steering wheel, listless in the traffic, flipping Jim the bird.

Jim was drifting, losing touch with reality, remembering something he'd written in his diary weeks before...

*Heading north into the orange-brown haze of the horizon. Cars transporting souls along a plane through time. Past and present merging in one stream of mind. Transporting me through several lifetimes. When I was a sailor, a wandering monk, a...a...CONCUBINE?!*

*"Oh, my God!"*

Jim slowly, carefully opened the door. Ariel smiled. "Leaving so soon? Thanks for dropping by. You really should go see the Expo. Great channeling," she said in a disarmingly sane manner.

Jim stepped out of the Pontiac with Nurse cupped in his arm and walked carefully around the car, still wearing the quartz. He stood motionless in the heat until Econoline inched by his side. And then he stepped in.

Mike didn't say a word.

Jim looked at Michael and handed him the rose quartz. "Here, I think you'd better put these on. I can't explain it, but that was one of the weirdest things that's ever happened to me." Jim's eyes bulged in their sockets....

"Mike, you know something, this journey is a *trip*!"

*James Crotty and Michael Lane (the Monks) are the publishers and editors of* Monk, the Mobile Magazine, *and are the authors of* The Mad Monks' Guide to New York City, The Mad Monks' Guide to California, Pink Highways, How to Talk American, *and* Mad Monks On the Road, *from which this story was excerpted. They are the hosts of the broadband/TV show,* Get Monked!: Around the World in a 26-Foot Motor Home, Covering 53 Countries, 26 Languages, in 48 Episodes, Returning to Hollywood Tweaked, Transformed, and Ready to Do Lunch. *Their web site is at www.Monk.com, and they can be reached at Monk@Monk.com.*

## A Past Life

*The wheels of karma go*
*round and round.*

WE LEFT DARJEELING NEXT MORNING ON A BRIGHT-BLUE toy train. The winding, narrow-gauge track crossed the road 132 unprotected times, on the seventy-five mile trip to New Jaipalguri. Consequently we were beset by a festival of warning bells, toots and whistles at each crossing. Although the train managed about nine miles an hour overall, it dragged along at snail's pace around curves and corkscrew loops. We were happy to have fresh whole wheat bread and tangerines stashed in our backpacks.

It was a grand winter morning when the train tooted from the station. Icy mountain air filled our lungs, and we leaned from the windows to imprint memories of Old Cart Road and the Elgin Hotel. Betsi raised her head high to view the last Kanchenjunga horizon and dropped expected tears in her handkerchief. She scrubbed them away with a firm knuckle and moment later smiled brightly. "I liked Darjeeling best of all," she said seriously. She had observed the same about Hong Kong, Bangkok, and Kashmir.

The little undisciplined train slowly struggled uphill and staggered five miles into the highest railway station in the world at Ghoom. We bought hot milk tea and popcorn from a semiliterate huckster and watched the monks blow their ceremonial horns. Then, in an agitated way, the steam engine groaned and squawked for a kilometer or so and settled down to a reluctant morning of servitude belching black cinders into our open car.

The circuitous journey included four complete loops and five switchbacks. Settlers had built huts within a few feet of the narrow track, so smells of morning breakfast wafted through open windows. Children hitched rides from their front doors, and delirious dogs nipped at the train in compulsive frenzy. At one corkscrew turn, Betsi, overcome with the carnival atmosphere, leaped from the train and raced down the narrow path to ride with the engineer directly below. It was a lifelong ambition. The startled engineer spoke in Urdu, somehow convincing her it was no place for a lady. Red-faced and puffing, she climbed back into our car as it drifted by, facing amused Hindus sitting beside us.

Blood-red hammer-and-sickle campaign signs filled entire walls proclaiming Communist hopes in an upcoming election. A rare billboard told us:

Urinating in public is illegal.
USE NEAREST PUBLIC CONVENIENCE

It was useless information, for one person had occupied the only toilet since leaving Darjeeling. She looked sadly out the open window oblivious to loud knocking and suggestions from bladder-filled passengers.

A brooding, middle-aged Hindu joined us a few miles

down the track. Long black hair straggled underneath his white Congress cap, and his fierce moustache bristled when he breathed. He seemed obsessed with a mighty problem. Five large silver rings stiffened his right hand, the middle finger carrying two massive ornaments appearing like a cluster of semiprecious puppet heads. They flashed as he clenched his fist.

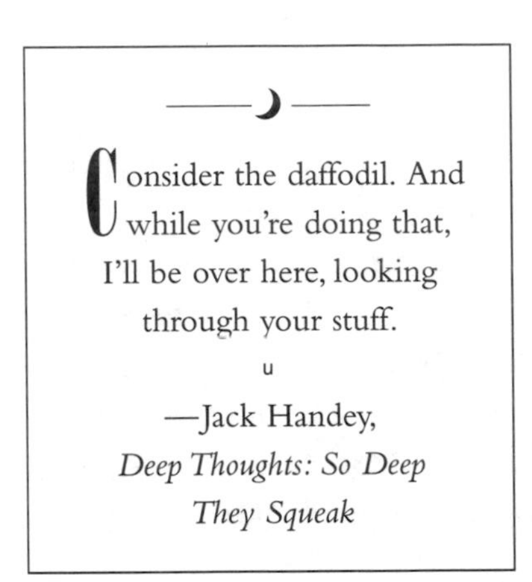

Consider the daffodil. And while you're doing that, I'll be over here, looking through your stuff.

—Jack Handey, *Deep Thoughts: So Deep They Squeak*

"Watch out for that one, he's got a tiger in his tank," Betsi whispered a warning.

The man's great brows lifted and glared at us. "You are looking...." he accused.

His jewelry rested less that a foot from my dazzled eyes. I blinked in fascination, for it appeared the grossest sort of ostentation. "Yes," I admitted. "Your rings invite inspection."

He observed my bare hands. "You are not wearing," he said.

"No, I am not wearing."

His lifted brows displayed suspicious brown eyes. "Why you are not wearing? You cannot afford?"

"In my country men do not wear many rings."

"It must be a very poor country."

"We are poor in many ways," I agreed, hoping it ended the conversation.

"India is overflowing with many riches." he said.

"We have observed your wealth in Delhi and are searching for further evidence in Calcutta tomorrow," Betsi replied.

She had just finished her last Snickers bar and prepared for withdrawal pain.

He shook his head quickly as if dodging small gnats, then pointed his finger at my nose. "Tell me," he said, "have we met in another world?"

"No, I think not," I replied slowly. "I would have remembered your rings."

"It is a possibility. You would be a difficult man to forget."

I turned to study the passing road traffic, hoping to terminate the conversation.

But he would not be put off. "Yes, that is true. I have an excellent mind and seem to remember you from the past." He glanced sideways at Betsi, but missed the glitter of her smirk.

Good manners prevented my telling him to buzz off, so I said, "If you recall where you knew me, please refresh my memory. My mind is not as clear as it was a few years ago." I hid behind a paperback.

The little engine led the train down winding tracks through pine forests and small hamlets. Sometimes we seemed almost to slip into the open houses as we rounded a bend. Women washed clothes and children played games apparently oblivious to our glances. Each time I lowered my book, I faced the intense black eyes of my neighbor staring with the concentration of a fanatic. By late afternoon the train trickled out of the mountains toward the valley of New Jaipalguri. The brooding Indian suddenly slapped his kneecap with a thunderous thump and said, "If you are concentrating we should have solved the mystery an hour ago. Are you yet remembering?"

"Answer the man," Betsi said, relishing my predicament. She told me later that she was interested in learning about my other lives, too.

"I cannot recall the exact place or time."

The Hindu flung his arms high. "It is mountainous area. You are happy, and young. Our fathers are friends. Now you are remembering?"

"Vaguely." It seemed sensible to agree.

He pounded my shoulder. "I knew I would remember. It was spring. The willows are budding, and we are walking to the working fields. Now you are remembering?"

The man's enthusiasm was so great that I saw his memories, too. "Yes, I am remembering!"

"In another world, you are my cousin Nimai!"

"And you were Pradib," I said, hoping the lie would end his fantasy.

"The name is close enough." The man leaped up and embraced me. We stood patting each other. Fortunately the train arrived at New Jaipalguri station, and passengers sorted luggage and children and, like a small riot, pushed through the narrow doors. "I will see you," I said.

"We must not wait so long next time." His great turquoise rings flashed in the sun.

"No, I promise."

He clasped me to his chest. "Good-bye, Nimai. Remember me to your father."

"I will never forget you, Pradib," I said. The man loosened his grip and disappeared into the moving crowd.

I fastened my backpack. "Take me home, Betsi. I've been here too long."

"I've said that for four months," she muttered.

I patted my hip pocket and keened the cry of an anguished widow. "The son of a bitch was a pickpocket," I yelped. "He stole my fake billfold, the one with news clippings in it. I hope he enjoys the three-year-old report on screw worms."

There was a pause while Betsi enjoyed my misery. I added, "It's hard to believe he did it. He's part of the family. We're relatively honest. You know."

Betsi smiled. "Humph. His rings were phony too. Like some of your relatives."

"Really?"

"Pure glass."

"Well, I'll be dammed. Can't even trust my own cousin."

"I'd watch out for his father in Calcutta if I were you."

*Dr. Burley Packwood is a retired dentist and World War II veteran who grew up along the Yellowstone River in Billings, Montana. He is the author of* Quail in My Bed *and* Bird Turd Peppers and Other Delights, *from which this story was excerpted.*

*

I recently returned to Kathmandu after living in America for many years. Before settling in, I spent a month of slothful travel in surreal India, around Delhi, Goa, Cochin, Ooty, Mysore, Bangalore, and Jaipur. I was reminded that in this part of the world nothing can be taken for granted. Anything important must be sent by registered mail, otherwise there's "no chance," as an attendant on the train to Cochin said every time I asked him for something that was due us as paying customers.

"We don't have a blanket," I said, hopeful he would remedy the situation.

"Sorry, sir, no blanket today. Very sorry."

"And pillow covers?"

"Sorry, sir, you must forgive and forget."

"Surely a bed sheet?"

A gleaming smile and a crushing utterance: "No chance."

"And no one has cleared the garbage either. There are discarded food trays under our seats."

"Sorry, sir, no cleaner in the train just now."

"Later perhaps? Or tomorrow?"

That enigmatic wag of the head, the brilliant, blinding smile, and then the inevitable: "No chance!"

"Any chance we will arrive on time in Cochin tomorrow?" The train was running around five hours late.

The killer smile, and then both of us in unison: "NO CHANCE!"

—Rajendra S. Khadka, "No Chance"

# *Index of Contributors*


Adams, Douglas 82–85

Barley, Nigel 18, 48–50
Barry, Dave 165–168
Bass, Thomas A. 51
Bassett, Paul 11, 177
Blank, Jonah 175
Bryson, Bill 43–47
Burns, George 89

Cahill, Tim 152–159
Carwardine, Mark 82–85
Cotham, Frank 135
Coverly, Dave 12
Crotty, Jim 185–193

Dalrymple, William 52–53, 81
Davis, Peter 97, 102, 134
Delbanco, Nicholas 178–180
Deschner, Whit 159
Donleavy, J. P. 136–141

Elkjer, Thom 98–106
Epstein, Benita 123, 177

Ferrin, Lynn 111–113
Ferris, Stewart 11, 177
Flinn, John 124–128
Forsythe, Lee 9

Gough, Laurie 126

Handey, Jack 74, 118, 150, 196
Hester, Elliott Neal 7–11
Horwitz, Tony 57–58

Kamel, Mohammed 151
Katz, Donald 86–93
Kellett, Keith 128
Kelly, John 142
Kersten, Carool 6
Khadka, Rajendra S. 199–200

Lamott, Anne 20–27
Lane, Michael 185–193
Lansky, Doug 169–172
Lara, Adair 174–176

McEwen, Todd 78–81
Melville, Herman vii
Millar, Margaret 45

Newsham, Brad 85, 161–164

O'Hanlon, Redmond 109
O'Reilly, James 29, 95–97
O'Rourke, P. J. 50

Packwood, Burley 172–173, 194–199
Paskal, Cleo 148–151
Potts, Rolf 115–122

Roberts, Paul William 54
Rubin, Leigh 54, 159

Salzman, Mark 107–109
Sedaris, David 28–32
Sen, Sourav 34–38
Shames, Germaine W. 39–42
Soliski, Jim 122
Sterling, Richard 181–183

Tabachnick, Cara 143–147
Twohy, Mike 184

Urrea, Luis Alberto 55–57

Warner, Gary A. 129–134
Whamond, Dave 110
White, Jayce 13–18
White, Randy Wayne 59–77
Wood, John 1–5

Ziegler, Jack 19, 33

# *Acknowledgments*

"How I Killed Off My Ex-Wife" by John Wood originally appeared as "It's a Wonderful Wife" in the December 28, 1997 issue of *The Washington Post.* Copyright © 1997 by John Wood. Reprinted by permission of the author.

"Hold On to Your Lunch" by Elliott Neal Hester. Copyright © 1999 by Elliott Neal Hester. This story first appeared as "Flying the Queasy Skies" in SALON.com, at http://www.salon.com. Reprinted by permission of Elliott Neal Hester.

"Everybody's Got Glorious Hide Next to Me and My Monkey" by Jayce White published with permission from the author. Copyright © 2000 by Jayce White.

"The Aunties" by Anne Lamott excerpted from *Traveling Mercies: Some Thoughts on Faith* by Anne Lamott. Copyright © 1999 by Anne Lamott. Reprinted by permission of Pantheon Books, a division of Random House, Inc.

"Jesus Shaves" by David Sedaris excerpted from *Me Talk Pretty One Day* by David Sedaris. Copyright © 2000 by David Sedaris. Reprinted by permission of Little, Brown and Company (Inc.), and Don Congdon Associates, Inc.

"*Benvenuto in Italia!*" by Sourav Sen published with permission from the author. Copyright © 2000 by Sourav Sen.

"Mexican Mating Calls" by Germaine W. Shames published with permission from the author. Copyright © 1994 by Germaine W. Shames.

"What's Cooking?" by Bill Bryson excerpted from *I'm a Stranger Here Myself: Notes on Returning to America After Twenty Years Away* by Bill Bryson. Copyright © 1999 by Bill Bryson. Reproduced by permission of Broadway Books, a division of Random House, Inc., and Greene & Heaton, Ltd.

"The Dentist in Cameroon" by Nigel Barley excerpted from *The Innocent Anthropologist: Notes from a Mud Hut* by Nigel Barley. Copyright © 1983 by Nigel Barley. Published by Penguin Books, Ltd. Reprinted by permission of David Higham Associates.

"The Crafty Cousin" by William Dalrymple excerpted from *From the Holy Mountain: A Journey Among the Christians of the Middle East* by William Dalrymple. Copyright © 1997 by William Hamilton-Dalrymple. Reprinted by permission of Henry Holt and Company, LLC.

"Incident at San Antonio" by Luis Alberto Urrea excerpted from *By the Lake of Sleeping Children: The Secret Life of the Mexican Border* by Luis Alberto Urrea.

author. Copyright © 2000 by Brad Newsham.
"Welcome to Ireland" by Dave Barry originally appeared as "Cheers" by Dave Barry reprinted from the August 6, 1995 issue of *The Miami Herald*. Copyright © 1995 by Dave Barry. Reprinted by permission of the author.
"Bad Haircuts Around the World" by Doug Lansky published with permission from the author. Copyright © 2000 by Doug Lansky.
"Fear of Not Flying" by Adair Lara reprinted from the January 26, 1995 issue of *The San Francisco Chronicle*. Copyright © 1995 *The San Francisco Chronicle*. Reprinted with permission.
"April Fool" by Nicholas Delbanco excerpted from *Running in Place: Scenes from the South of France* by Nicholas Delbanco. Copyright © 1989 by Nicholas Delbanco. Used by permission of Grove/Atlantic, Inc.
"Mr. Disguise" by Richard Sterling published with permission from the author. Copyright © 2000 by Richard Sterling.
"Close Encounters of the California Kind" by Michael Lane and Jim Crotty excerpted from *Mad Monks on the Road* by Michael Lane and Jim Crotty. Copyright © 1993 by Fireside. Reprinted by permission.
"A Past Life" by Burley Packwood excerpted from *Bird Turd Peppers and Other Delights* by Burley Packwood. Copyright © 1993 by Burley Packwood. Reprinted by permission of Quantum Press of Arizona.

**Additional Credits (arranged alphabetically by title)**

Selection from "Aeroflotsam and Jetsam" by Lee Forysthe published with permission from the author. Copyright © 2000 by Lee Forsythe.
Selection from *Arrow of the Blue-Skinned God: Retracing the Ramayana through India* by Jonah Blank copyright © 1992 by Jonah Blank. Reprinted by permission of Houghton Mifflin Company. All rights reserved.
Selection from *Baghdad Without a Map, and Other Misadventures in Arabia* by Tony Horwitz copyright © 1991 by Tony Horwitz. Reprinted by permission of Penguin Putnam USA and Bloomsbury Publishing, Ltd.
Selection from "Baksheesh" by Keith Kellett published with permission from the author. Copyright © 2000 by Keith Kellett.
Selection from *Bird Turd Peppers and Other Delights* by Burley Packwood copyright © 1993 by Burley Packwood. Reprinted by permission of Quantum Press of Arizona.
Selection from *Camping with the Prince and Other Tales of Science in Africa* by Thomas A. Bass copyright © 1990 by Thomas A. Bass. Published by Houghton Mifflin. Reprinted by permission of the author.
Selection from *Congo Journey* by Redmond O'Hanlon, published in the United States as *No Mercy: A Journey Into the Heart of the Congo* copyright © 1996 by Redmond O'Hanlon. Reprinted by permission of Peters, Fraser & Dunlop Group.
Selection from *Cool About the Ankles* by John Kelly copyright © 1997 by John Kelly. Published by The Blackstaff Press Limited, Belfast, North Ireland.
Selection from *Deep Thoughts* by Jack Handey copyright © 1994 by Jack Handey. Published by Berkeley Publishing Group, a division of Penguin Putnam USA.

Seclection from Deep Thoughts Calendar 1995 by Jack Handey copyright © 1995 by Jack Handey. Published by Andrews McMeel Publishing, Kansas City. MO.

Selection from *Deeper Thoughts, All New, All Crispy* by Jack Handey copyright © 1993 by Jack Handey. Published by Hyperion, New York, NY.

Selection from *Deepest Thoughts, So Deep They Squeak* by Jack Handey copyright © 1994 by Jack Handey. Published by Hyperion, New York, NY.

Selection from "Does Your Meter Work?!" by Jim Soliski published with permission from the author. Copyright © 2000 by Jim Soliski.

Selections from *Don't Mention the War!: A Shameful European Adventure* by Stewart Ferris and Paul Bassett copyright © 1998 by Stewart Ferris and Paul Bassett. Published by Summersdale Publishers, Ltd., Chichester, West Sussex, UK.

Selection from *In Search of the Birth of Jesus: The Real Journey of the Magi* by Paul William Roberts copyright © 1995 by Paul William Roberts. Used by permission of Riverhead Books, a division of Penguin Putnam, Inc., and Stoddart Publishing Company, Ltd, Don Mills, Ontario.

Selection from *In Xanadu: A Quest* by William Dalrymple copyright © 1986 by William Dalrymple. Published by HarperCollins, Ltd., London.

Selection from *The Innocent Anthropologist: Notes from a Mud Hut* by Nigel Barley copyright © 1983 by Nigel Barley. Published by Penguin Books, Ltd. Reprinted by permission of David Higham Associates.

Selection from "It's Over" by P. J. O'Rourke reprinted from the November 1999 issue of *Men's Journal*. Copyright © 1999 by Men's Journal Company, L.P. All rights reserved. Reprinted by permission.

Selection from *Kite Strings of the Southern Cross: A Woman's Travel Odyssey* by Laurie Gough copyright © 1998 by Laurie Gough. Published in Canada as *Island of the Human Heart: A Woman's Travel Odyssey* by Turnstone Press. Reprinted by permission of Travelers' Tales, Inc. and Turnstone Press.

Selection from "My Son in Vietnam" by Carool Kersten published with permission from the author. Copyright © 2000 by Carool Kersten.

Selection from "No Chance" by Rajendra S. Khadka published with permission from the author. Copyright © 2000 by Rajendra S. Khadka.

Selections from "Room Checking" by Peter Davis published with permission from the author. Copyright © 2000 by Peter Davis.

Selections from *Take Me with You: A Round-the-World Journey to Invite a Stranger Home* by Brad Newsham copyright © 2000 by Brad Newsham. Reprinted by permission of Travelers' Tales, Inc.

Selection from *Travels with a Kayak* by Whit Deschner copyright © 1997. Published by The Eddie Tern Press, Baker, OR.

Selection from "Troglodytes in Gaul" by James O'Reilly reprinted from *Travelers' Tales France* edited by James O'Reilly, Larry Habegger, and Sean O'Reilly. Copyright © 1995 by Travelers' Tales, Inc. Reprinted by permission of the author.

Selection from "You Don't Choose Your Travel Companions" by Peter Davis published with permission from the author. Copyright © 2000 by Peter Davis.

**Cartoons Credits (arranged alphabetically by artist)**

Drawing by Frank Cotham originally appeared in June 8, 1998 issue of Barron's. Copyright © 1998 by Frank Cotham. Reprinted by permission of the artist.
Drawings by Dave Coverly copyright © 1999 by Dave Coverly. Reprinted by permission of Dave Coverly and Creators Syndicate.
Drawings by Benita Epstein copyright © 2000 by Benita Epstein. Reprinted by permission of the artist. www.reuben.org/benitaepstein. Benitae@aol.com
Drawings by Leigh Rubin copyright © 1998 by Leigh Rubin. Reprinted by permission of Leigh Rubin and Creators Syndicate.
Drawing by Mike Twohy copyright © 2000 The New Yorker Collection from cartoonbank.com. All Rights Reserved.
Drawing by Dave Whamond. Reality Check©UFS. Reprinted by permission.
Drawings by Jack Ziegler "King Kong" and "A Sudden Realization" from Hamburger Madness, copyright © 1978 by Jack Ziegler, reproduced by permission of Harcourt, Inc.

# *About the Editor*

Tim Cahill is the author of nine books, mostly travel related, including *Jaguars Ripped My Flesh, Pecked to Death by Ducks, Hold the Enlightenment,* and *Lost in my Own Backyard.* He describes what he does for a living as "remote journeys, oddly rendered." Reviewers have been overwhelmingly kind, though some have accused him of committing humor on occasion. Cahill is also the co-author of the Academy Award-nominated IMAX films *The Living Sea* and *Dolphins,* as well as the highly acclaimed *Everest.* He lives in Montana with his wife Linnea Larson, two dogs, two cats, and a host of friends who also seem to believe that he has a sense of humor. Either that or they just spend a lot of time laughing at him.